BOLD
Mission

BOLD Mission

Courageously Pursue Your Calling

DEBRA BOBLITT

NICHE PRESSWORKS

Published by Niche Pressworks; http://NichePressworks.com
Indianapolis, IN

ISBN-13: 978-1-952654-62-6 Paperback
978-1-952654-67-1 Hardback
978-1-952654-63-3 eBook

Printed in the United States of America

Foreword

The philosopher Soren Kierkegaard (1813–55) mused, "What I really need is to arrive at a clear comprehension of what I am to do ... to find the idea for which I am willing to live and to die."[1]

By Kierkegaard's standard, most of us aren't doing very well, and it seems to worsen with each generation. Seventy-five percent of young adults say they do not have a sense of purpose that gives them meaning in life. Half say they regularly struggle with anxiety and depression.[2]

When it comes to the value of our work, the news is even tougher. In 2021, the Gallup polling organization surveyed workers in 160 countries and found that seven in ten employees are "struggling or suffering, rather than thriving, in their overall lives." Eighty percent lack a sense of engagement.[3]

Surveys like these make me wonder, "How is it that what we spend most of our waking hours doing sucks the life out of us?"

This isn't just a question of personal fulfillment. It's a question of truth. If truth is up to each individual (which is what the majority believes), and we aren't achieving what we'd like, then it must be that we are controlled by fate. We are victims.

Debra Boblitt refuses to accept this diagnosis. In *Bold Mission,* she demonstrates with examples from her own life and career — and from the inspiring examples of her coaching clients — that we can live differently. Bold Mission is full of step-by-step strategies to strengthen your sense of mission, analyze and overcome your fears, and live a more fulfilling life.

I especially appreciate how Debra weaves together work life and spiritual life. Truly successful people learn how to shape their outward circumstances by carefully cultivating what is inside. No matter where you are spiritually, this is a valuable lesson for us all.

In my career as a professor, business owner, and non-profit leader, I've learned that having an inspiring sense of mission isn't something that happens all at once. It's an intentional choice to think differently about each decision we make. Some decisions seem inconsequential, but over time, our responses reveal a pattern. *Bold Mission* shows you how to change that pattern for the better.

Imagine what kind of world this would be if we each learned to move forward rather than backward, engage rather than escape, and build up rather than tear down.

As I read *Bold Mission*, I was reminded of the beloved poem "Psalm of Life" by Henry Wadsworth Longfellow.[4] Here are my favorite lines:

> *Lives of great men all remind us*
> *We can make our lives sublime,*
> *And, departing, leave behind us*
> *Footprints on the sands of time;*
> *Footprints, that perhaps another,*
> *Sailing o'er life's solemn main,*
> *A forlorn and shipwrecked brother,*
> *Seeing, shall take heart again.*
> *Let us, then, be up and doing,*
> *With a heart for any fate;*
> *Still achieving, still pursuing,*
> *Learn to labor and to wait.*

We only get a certain number of days on this planet. *Bold Mission* reveals that our Creator has given us the resources we need to make the most of our days to pursue flourishing and blessing.

I hope you enjoy *Bold Mission* and take its lessons to heart. Now is the time to be B.O.L.D.!

Jeff Myers, PhD
President, Summit Ministries, and
Author, *Truth Changes Everything*

Table of Contents

Chapter 1

Introduction

"**J**ust tell me what the problem is."

I sat across the desk from my manager. Just a few weeks before, he had told me I was being considered for a promotion, one that would mark a big step forward on my career path at the Fortune 50 financial services company I worked for. His eyes moved around the room, obviously trying to avoid resting on me. For the past week, he'd hinted that there was a snag, something that was standing in the way of this next step on the ladder of achievement I so badly wanted — and deserved.

"Well," he said, "to be blunt ..." he trailed off, again avoiding my eyes.

Yes, please be blunt! I wanted to shout. *I'm Italian! I can take it — just tell me!* Whatever the issue was with my pending promotion, I wanted it straight — even if it meant leaping across the desk and shaking it out of him. Instead, though, I waited patiently. I took a deep breath and sat up as straight as possible, trying to look taller than my five foot, two inches. He shifted in his chair again and moved some papers around on his desk.

Finally, he opened his mouth. "You know that you're qualified for this position. But some people have concerns about … well, about your hair."

Out of all the things I thought could possibly derail my career plans, my hair didn't even show up on the list. This was the 1990s, so being a woman was still seen by many as a disadvantage to overcome. I also had a nontraditional background, coming from education rather than business. But my numbers showed I could do the job and do it well. I could hardly believe that the thing standing in my way now was … *my hair?!*

I won't bore you with the details of the vehement yet respectful discussion that followed. Suffice it to say, I defended myself, my record, and my hair — and got the promotion. I left that office with my dignity intact but with a few more scars from the battle.

That incident was not an isolated blip on my journey up the corporate ladder. From my clothing to my personality to my passion, it all was critiqued … and not always positively. People often ask what got me through the tough times and allowed me to continue to embrace what I knew was my calling, despite the myriad challenges along the way. The answer is twofold:

First, I don't back down from a challenge. Second, I knew that I could do great things for the organization, my team, and our clients. I was on a mission, and if I had to face down a few dozen naysayers along the way, so be it. My purpose was bigger than the obstacles I faced, bigger than my fears … even bigger than my hair!

As I look back over my thirty years at the highest organizational levels, I realize that my time in corporate America coincided with the growing presence of women executives, the Internet, the emergence of "work-life balance," and the desire for work to reflect something beyond a paycheck. Now, it is unthinkable to admit out loud that someone's personal appearance might be the reason for their failure to advance.

But I'd argue that, as a culture, we are facing even more dire pressures. In the wake of the global pandemic, civil unrest, huge disparities among social groups, and growing tension at home and abroad, we are in desperate need of leaders — bold leaders, ones who feel deeply called to set aside personal agendas in favor of helping to heal our struggling nation.

Throughout my career in corporate America and now as a business coach and speaker, I've seen the bad and good of leadership. I've witnessed good people with wonderful ideas who couldn't move their plans forward because of a lack of resources or vision. I've watched others with fantastic leadership skills lead their teams in the wrong direction. I've seen individuals with powerful dreams step back out of fear of rejection or failure. My mission, whether in the workplace or individually, is to develop leaders to pursue their own bold dreams. That's why I feel called to share my lessons in this book. Quite simply, I want to equip others to lead courageously in a world that so desperately needs people of character to step out and speak up.

The deck is stacked against those of us who question the common narrative and refuse to blindly believe what the media tells us. All the institutions we trusted with our money and our lives have failed us, yet they still want us to keep our mouths shut and our wallets open. Diversity of appearance is encouraged, yet diversity of thought is squelched, to the detriment of our businesses, our government, and our culture. But things don't have to be like that.

In the pages of this book, I've distilled my decades of experience and education into a simple, four-part formula for bringing your bold dream to life:

B: Believing It
O: Owning It
L: Living It
D: Duplicating It

We'll talk about the concrete steps you'll need to go from idea to actuality, including determining your unique mission, amassing resources, planning your execution, dealing with setbacks and struggles, sharing your ideas, enlisting support, and more.

To illustrate the lessons you'll learn, you'll hear much about my personal story. I'll also introduce you to courageous men and women who decided their personal callings were too important to put on the back burner and too needed to ignore. They've generously agreed to share their personal struggles and successes with you. They know how helpful it can be to hear from someone else who has walked a similar path, particularly during the tough times.

Speaking of tough times, you might be wondering if the risk is worth the reward. I — and everyone else whose stories I share in this book — would answer with a resounding "Yes!" For people like us, the choice between staying silent and small and living for what we believe in is clear. We know that by living boldly, we are not only standing up in favor of transforming our environment, we are also creating a legacy of which we can be proud.

If you cannot quiet the tug on your heart that pulls you to something bigger, welcome. This book is for you. Your life of purpose awaits.

BELIEVE IT

After working with thousands of salespeople, executives, and entrepreneurs, both as a leader in corporate management and as a coach, I can say with complete confidence that you *are* here for a reason, a unique purpose only you can fulfill. I have never met a person without a God-given mission — even if they couldn't see it themselves. While your mission can be hidden, unclear, or lost for a time, never doubt that it exists. And it's up to you (with my help!) to uncover it.

If you don't quite buy into that yet, I get it. There was a time in my life when I was lost, and I literally didn't know what I was supposed to do next. I questioned my path and my purpose. As a goal-oriented, Type-A person who was always looking to the next challenge, I was very uncomfortable not knowing if I was headed in the right direction.

At the time, I was well into my career in education administration and making progress toward my PhD, but something was off. During my student teaching, I remember standing in front of the classroom thinking, *"I just don't think I can do this for the rest of my life."* I was doing what I'd prepared for years to do and what I thought I was supposed to do ... but it didn't fit, and that was scary.

"What am I meant to be? What am I meant to do?" I asked myself — and God — over and over. If I wasn't meant to be in education (and each day made me more and more convinced that I wasn't), where did I belong? What would I be and what would I do if I chose not to continue on this path I'd thought was set for me? If I was going to go in another direction, I wanted a clear road map — a new destination I could plug into my mental GPS and head off to with confidence and efficiency. Without a concrete path, I felt adrift and very, very insecure.

I think every intelligent person reaches a point like this where we question our existence. We wonder if we're on the right path, on the wrong path, or if there's a path at all. Despite how uncomfortable it can feel, I believe it's actually a sign of growth and maturity to reach a point where we realize life is finite and we have the desire to make the most of what's been given to us in the time we have.

One of the big pitfalls, though, is confusing the "what" with the "if." Here's what I mean: Don't let doubt about your life's path fool you into thinking that your mission doesn't exist. Just because you're not sure WHAT your mission is, doesn't mean there isn't one! You don't lack purpose. Instead, what you lack is clarity. Some of history's greatest leaders and thinkers at times questioned their calling. From Moses to Mother Teresa, from George Washington to Jackson Pollack, uncertainty and doubt often go along with having a bold mission.

There's a big difference between wondering if you have a purpose and wondering what that purpose is. When you know you have a purpose (even a yet-to-be-discovered one), you can move forward with:

- Intention
- Curiosity
- Excitement
- Courage
- Energy

So here's what I ask of you. For the duration of this book, proceed from the assumption that you ARE here for a reason and that you just need time, space, and guidance to figure out what it is. Don't doubt your value, worth, or uniqueness. Take them as a given.

As the Psalmist writes in the Old Testament,

For you created my inmost being;
you knit me together in my mother's womb.
I praise you because I am fearfully and wonderfully made;
your works are wonderful,

I know that full well.
My frame was not hidden from you
when I was made in the secret place,
when I was woven together in the depths of the earth.
Your eyes saw my unformed body;
all the days ordained for me were written in your book
before one of them came to be.
                                        –Psalm 139:13-16, NIV

If you're not a student of the Bible, it may be difficult for you to believe that you were uniquely and wonderfully created for a specific purpose. But if you can proceed from this foundation, you can go through the following chapters with a spirit of exploration and energy rather than depression and doubt.

I'll be sharing more of my own journey of discovery in this book, but for now, I'll share that questioning my purpose was one of the best things I have ever done — both as an individual and as a leader. The process led me to deeper levels of commitment and intention, something bold leaders need.

Now, let's focus on how you can BELIEVE your Bold Mission. In this section, you'll learn how knowing your values (your nonnegotiables and priorities) combines with your gifts to generate a mission only YOU can fulfill. You'll see how what's happened to you in your life so far has contributed to a set of skills and experiences that have equipped you for your Bold Mission. Ready?

Chapter 2

Building Your Foundation: Values

Our world seems to be getting crazier and less certain day by day. Things we took for granted in my childhood — respect for each other, respect for our police, the exceptional nature of our country, and biological differences between men and women, to name just a few — are now open for interpretation, at least according to the mainstream media. The parameters we had around so much of our life have disappeared, with nothing to replace them except what's trending on Twitter or what gets the most likes on TikTok.

The pandemic of 2020 made people question institutions we'd long trusted to have our best interests at heart. It was like scales had fallen from our eyes, and many of the structures we'd counted on to protect us fell apart.

When the world around you is in such disarray, and there are no longer any boundaries, it becomes hard to find your footing. When you're in a position of leadership, that sense of uncertainty can be even more pronounced. How can you serve as a model for others when you, yourself, are unsure?

That's why it's so critical to start with what you know to be true. When I'm working with a coaching client, one of the first things we do is talk about values. I want to know what is most important to them. I want to know who they are at their core. What about them is absolute, permanent, and never-changing?

The Bible talks about a foolish man who built his house on the sand in the book of Matthew. When the storms came and the waters rose, the house was unable to stand because its foundation was built on the shifting sands. In contrast, the wise man built his house on rock. Because of this firm foundation, even when the storms came, the house still stood.

Being a leader is like building a house. You are going to face storms of criticism, uncertainty, and challenges of all kinds. But if your mission is built on a strong, unchanging foundation, you will have nothing to fear.

What Are Values?

Your values are your priorities, the things in your life you focus on. The funny thing about values is that they are in the background of everything you do, whether or not you know it. Even if you don't consciously think about your values, every decision you make has to do with what your basic values are.

Your basic values typically do not change over the course of your life, though the expression of them may change a bit. For instance, my top values include faith, courage, integrity, authenticity, and freedom. While they may come out in different ways, they've been there for most, if not all, of my life.

Values are critical because they become the lens through which you see the world and through which you make decisions. If a decision is going to require that you betray or violate a value, that would be a hard no.

This became all too real to me when I was asked to evaluate a decision the member of the chairman's office of my company had proposed for the entire United States. As soon as I heard about the proposal, I had some serious misgivings. I didn't say anything right away because I wanted to confirm my gut reaction. My team and I did some research, and sure enough, the CEO's proposal was going to be problematic from a number of perspectives. I then had a choice: I could keep my mouth shut and just go with the flow, helping to roll out this disastrous program ... Or I could march myself upstairs and tell the cabinet that this proposal, their new baby, was ugly.

It didn't take me long to make that decision. Even if it meant that I would be rejected, demoted, or even let go, I couldn't keep my mouth shut (hey, I'm Italian!). I had the stats and research to back up my position, so upstairs I went, presentation in hand. I told the CEO and his team what I knew to be true, what my concerns were, and why this program wasn't in the best interests of the company long-term. They were silent for a bit, thanked me for my input, and then I went back downstairs.

I didn't hear much more about it, but I didn't get fired, so I counted that as a win! But not even a month later, I got a phone call while I was in my office downstairs, and I was told I was being promoted — largely because I was willing to look the CEO in the eye and tell him the truth when everyone around him was scared to push back. In fact, at other points in my career, I was told I was selected for specific assignments over other very qualified candidates because of my reputation for boldness.

There are times when I was rewarded for sticking to my values … but don't get fooled into thinking you'll always get rewarded or celebrated for being a person of integrity. In fact, in today's culture, it's just as likely that you'll be attacked for standing up for what's right. But external approval isn't the point. That is transitory. What's "in" one day is "out" the next. That's why it's so critical to know who you are and what you stand for.

Knowing what is important to you grounds you. No matter what happens in life, at the end of the day, you can rest your head on your pillow because you've lived in alignment with your values. If I had gotten fired for going toe-to-toe with the CEO, I would have left with my head held high. And if I'd gotten a promotion for going along with the plan when I knew in my heart it wasn't the right thing to do, that new title and salary would have been meaningless. The peace that comes from living in accordance with my values is something that cannot be bought or sold.

How Do You Know What Your Values Are?

Now that you have an idea of what values are and why they're important, you're probably wondering how to figure out what your values are. Some people intuitively know what matters most to them. Maybe you've done a leadership program or some other type of personal development course where you've looked at your values. There are a lot of online, interactive values assessments. Just google "free values assessment," and you'll get a bunch of options. These can be valuable, but they can also get a little predictable and stilted (who is NOT going to say, "I value honesty?!").

This is such an important topic that it merits a little deeper work. After all, it's the foundation from which everything else will be built!

If we were working together one-on-one, I'd ask you to tell me all about yourself, including your successes, what you consider to be failures, important decisions you've made, and more. After spending time with you and hearing you talk, I'd get an intuitive hit as to your priorities and values and a sense of how strongly you feel about certain topics.

Because we can't do that here, I've developed two exercises to help you do this process on your own.

1. Looking Back to Look Forward

For this exercise, you're going to review some big decisions you've made in your life. Pick significant times when you were choosing between two (or more) paths. Here is a list of possible decisions to get you thinking in the right direction:

- Choosing one job offer over another
- Choosing where to attend college
- Choosing an internship
- Choosing what to study in school
- Choosing whether to go to grad school or go to work
- Choosing what city to move to

We're looking for three to five decisions that could have changed the course of your life if not completely, then to a consequential degree, and, ideally, decisions where you had to weigh different priorities.

Once you've got a list, go through each decision, one at a time. Ask yourself the following questions, and write down the answers (as tempting as it may be to try to do this in your head, don't. Take the time to put it all down in writing.):

- What were my options?
- Why was this decision hard (or easy) to make?
- What was the determining factor?
- What values were coming into play or were in conflict with each other?
- Why did you finally choose the way you did?
- In retrospect, are you happy with this decision? Why or why not?

Now, spend some time reviewing your answers. Look for patterns. Did you always choose the option that would give you greater freedom? Did you "go with your gut?" Do you regret times when you chose comfort over adventure or pleasing others instead of doing what you knew you wanted? Jot down as many "Ahas" as you can. I bet there are some big clues to your values hidden in these answers!

Note: This is an exercise you can do over and over. In fact, it's a great process to go through when you make a big decision. Your goal, over time, is to become more clear about your values and make decisions in line with those values.

2. *Looking Forward to Look Back*

In the first exercise, I asked you to look to the past. In this exercise, we're going to look to the future. There's a popular exercise you may have done before in a seminar where you are asked to write your obituary. The idea is that by thinking about what people will say about you after you die, you can bring your current life in line with your ideal outcome (your legacy).

This exercise is similar but with a little lighter twist. Rather than pretending you've died (which might be a little depressing), I'd like you to think twenty, thirty, or even fifty years from now when you are still very much alive, and you're considering the legacy you've created in your time on earth. Consider the following questions:

- What have you spent your time, treasures, and talents creating?
- Who have you helped?
- What problem(s) did you solve?
- What are you known for?
- What do people come to you for?
- What are you most proud of?
- Who do you spend time with?

Again, write it all out ... and then review your answers for patterns.

I like the combination of these two exercises because one is based on what actually happened in the past, and one is based on your dreams for the future. By combining the two together, you can get an excellent picture of where you've been, where you want to go, and what you may need to change now, in the present, to get to your desired outcome.

My Foundation

I couldn't end this chapter without sharing with you the source of my values, which is my faith. As a Christian, I believe that the Bible is the unerring word of God. What he has given us in the Old and New Testaments is truth yesterday, today, and forever. I can't overstate how much peace this gives me in an uncertain and ever-changing world.

When I faced my own period of wondering what I was created for back in my late 20s, it was my relationship with God that guided me. I returned to the promise of Psalm 139, which I shared with you earlier, over and over again. I knew that God had created me for a purpose, and I needed only to walk in faith toward the future he had created for me.

If you are not a Christian and would like to learn more about Jesus, know this: God gave his son for you so that you can have everlasting life (John 3:16). Trust me ... When you view your days through this perspective, it changes everything.

Chapter 3

What Are You Made Of?

H ere's something you might not have thought about when it comes to your life purpose: You are in training. You are sharpening your skills, increasing your abilities, and building mental and emotional muscle.

Think about it. The military spends months upon months drilling for a relatively limited time in battle. Athletes spend most of their time practicing, lifting weights, stretching, and otherwise improving their strength and skill, so they are ready for game day.

Likewise, you also are preparing. Living boldly, by definition, requires courage and confidence, strength and stamina. As a leader, you're a focus point for attention and criticism — particularly when what you have to say may go against popular opinion. I bet that you've already picked up on this fact. Anytime you step outside the ordinary and strive for something else, you'll be faced with obstacles, challenges, and distractions — internal and external.

Everyone I introduce you to through the pages of this book is an example of pursuing their mission despite incredible barriers. There's Ericka, a single mom who was determined to open her own nail salon despite COVID shutdowns, financial challenges, and more. There's Michelle, who faced multiple health challenges and still went on to establish a well-regarded nonprofit helping other mothers in times of crisis. There's Martha, who overcame domestic abuse and lack of education to create not one but four successful businesses and earn the Champion of Freedom award. There's Nathan (you'll learn more about him later in this chapter), who has had to stand up to the medical establishment to advocate for patient health.

Don't be put off by the challenges. Every single one of these people would tell you that not only is it personally fulfilling to live courageously, but that the world also needs you and your voice. And I guarantee that you've already amassed a collection of talents and skills that will help you successfully bring your message to the world. In this chapter, we'll take a look at what's already in your toolkit.

Gifts and Skills — The Seed and the Vine

It's always exciting for me to see how the seeds of my clients' gifts and talents were planted long ago and how their strengths bloomed over time to be called into service as they pursue their purpose. Nothing is accidental. When you were created, God knew exactly what you'd need to fulfill your calling.

I'm a perfect example. As long as I can remember, I have been known for being the organizer in any group. The third of four girls, I automatically stepped in to lead the effort when something had to get done. From teaching my younger sister to tie her shoes to reading *Pippi Longstocking* at bedtime, I easily and naturally pulled people together to unite around a goal, assigned responsibilities, and kept everyone motivated and on track.

Based on my natural skills, it was not a surprise to any of my family members or friends when, a few decades later, I performed the same role in the corporate world. As I pursued my own calling, I called upon all these talents and abilities to inspire, support, and motivate others. I needed the organizational skills to help my team members improve their performance. I needed my natural enthusiasm and energy when times were tough. I needed my ability to bring people together when there were disagreements about the proper course of action. The seeds of my success as an executive — and now as a coach and speaker — were born in those early days.

But seeds need to be watered and tended to grow. Yes, I was organized, intelligent, and energetic from an early age. But if I'd never invested in those gifts, they would have remained undeveloped, like tiny, green plant shoots that were never given the sunshine or water needed to grow sturdy vines.

I had to invest in developing my skills through effort, experimentation, and even failure. Without working to develop those abilities, I might have still been able to "lead" my friends, but I wouldn't have had the wisdom or experience to lead a nationwide team. Maybe I would have been able to read a bedtime story and entertain my sister, but I wouldn't have had the competence or confidence to stand on a stage in front of thousands of people and move them with my words.

I didn't become an expert overnight; it took many years, much trial and error, and a lot of hard work (often when I didn't feel like it!) to create an expertise I could count on. My gifts had to be tended to and cared for so I could later call upon them when I became an executive, a mentor, and a coach and speaker, helping others identify greatness within themselves. I would be much less effective if I had not invested in my gifts.

Another example is my client Nathan. With an early interest in and aptitude for science and holding a deep respect for human life, he has always been enthralled with the world around him. From a young age, he wanted to learn more about the functioning of the human body. That interest was not only a gift from God, it was also a huge road sign as to where he would eventually find his purpose. The seed had been planted in his childhood, and Nathan watered and fertilized it through years of schooling and practice. Now he spends his days as an integrative oncology expert, studying the impact of high-dose Vitamin C on cancer and helping his patients extend their lives despite their diagnoses.

Start thinking about your seeds and which vines you see growing in your life. Just like with Nathan and with me, these early clues can be clear indications of where your purpose lies. When we start looking at your specific mission, we'll take stock of your strengths as well as your values and see how you are moved to put your unique personality and preferences to use on behalf of the larger world. As you'll see in the next chapter, it is so satisfying to see how it all comes together, even if the edges are fuzzy at first.

Claiming Your Strengths

As a Christian, I believe that God gives us talents and gifts specifically so we can put them to use on behalf of others. Yes, it's wonderful to have the potential to be a powerful public speaker, but that talent means nothing if it's not used to better the lives of others. Hitler and Lincoln were both persuasive speakers. One used his power for evil and destruction, while the other used it to unite and heal a country. Similarly, Nathan could have directed his interests and talents in a number of different ways, but he felt compelled to help others heal and to alleviate suffering.

It's common to examine your skills and talents and think that they aren't as valuable or important as, say, healing people. Or you look at your abilities and think, "Well, that's not too impressive. Anyone can do that." If this is you ... stop! The strengths you possess have gotten you to where you are today, and they are preparing you for your future calling. Just as Nathan's skills and interests equip him to effectively treat his patients, yours enable you to do something unique to your life goals. Not everyone can (or should) be a doctor, just as not everyone can (or should) be a pastor, an author, a teacher, or an entrepreneur.

You are here for a specific purpose, one that is as critical to the world as anyone else's. Never doubt that. Without your contributions, something would be missing! There's a passage in the book of 1 Corinthians in the Bible that speaks to this need for all of our skills and talents:

> *If the whole body were an eye, how could it hear? If the whole body were an ear, how could it smell? God has placed each part in the body just as he wanted it to be. If all the parts were the same, how could there be a body?*
>
> –1 Cor. 12:17-19, NIV

In other words, we are all part of a whole. What you contribute is needed — believe it!

Maybe you know you're darned good at what you do, but you've been reluctant to openly claim it. Despite knowing you are talented, you're not sure how to let others know about your skills without being seen as a braggart or full of yourself. You need to not only know what you're capable of, but you have to be willing to claim it as well.

Claiming your expertise is something that can be tough, especially for women. We tend to hide our abilities, knowledge, and strengths for fear we'll be seen as full of ourselves or stuck up.

I personally had to learn the difference between "bragging" and "confidence," and there's a huge difference between the two. Whether it was on my website, in interviews, or on my resume, I had to learn how to share my accomplishments, skills, and talents in a way that showed confidence. The best way to claim your abilities is to have data to back up your skills. If you can illustrate what you've accomplished and back it up with facts, it won't be perceived as bragging — it's just the truth!

Think of it this way: If you don't believe in and claim your expertise, who will miss out? When you believe in your skills and describe them with legitimate confidence, you make yourself available to help someone — or your entire organization — achieve their goals.

If Michelle hadn't believed she could help other mothers, hundreds of women and their families would have missed out on the support from her nonprofit.

If Ericka hadn't believed she had the ability to be a business owner, her family would have suffered, and she wouldn't have been able to pamper hundreds of clients with her special brand of customer service.

If Martha hadn't believed she had worth and value, hundreds of her employees would not have achieved self-sufficiency.

If Nathan hadn't believed he was meant to stand for health freedom, thousands of patients with cancer wouldn't have access to life-saving and life-prolonging therapies.

And if I hadn't believed I had expertise to share, you wouldn't be reading this book right now!

You also have a role to play in healing, supporting, and impacting others around you. You just have to believe it.

Digging Deep

Hopefully, through the course of this chapter, you've started to think back to some of your early interests and skills. In this section, I'll help you dig a little deeper to figure out what skills and talents you possess that may be called into use as you pursue your purpose. Use these questions as prompts. You may want to jot answers down in a journal or a computer file or talk through them with a trusted friend, mentor, or coach.

- **What have you always loved to do? What were your early interests, abilities, and passions?**
  Think about Nathan's interest in the human body or my early signs of leadership.

- **What do you get complimented on? What do other people openly admire about you?**

  These don't necessarily have to be directly related to your career. Knowing that others love how you always make them feel welcome in your home could point to your ability to connect with others.

- **What experiences have you had in your life that have called on you to develop specific skills?**

  Maybe you are the oldest of six kids or you worked your way through college as a customer service rep. Those experiences taught you some valuable skills!

- **What do you already know you are good, great, or excellent at? What data or facts do you have to back up that knowledge?**

  Knowing and believing your value is easier when you have proof.

In the next chapter, we'll start putting this all together to identify your unique mission.

Chapter 4

Putting It All Together

In this chapter, we'll look at how to zero in on your unique path.

So far, we've been talking about your "mission" as if it's a secret assignment, passed to you in a metal briefcase and protected by a code that only you know, like something out of *Mission: Impossible*. Sure, there may be some rare people who have one fixed purpose in life that they are laser-focused on from day one. But for most of us, our purpose in life is a lot less clear and includes what may look like dead ends and false starts.

If you are less than crystal-clear on your calling, you're in good company. Virtually every person you will meet in this book went on a journey of discovery before feeling like they were truly living their mission. Often, that journey has a lot of twists and turns, as the story of Joseph in the book of Genesis in the Old Testament demonstrates.

I won't go through all his ups and downs here, but before he came into his God-given mission, he was:

- Sold into slavery by his brothers
- Sold again to Pharaoh, the leader of Egypt
- Wrongly accused of rape by Pharaoh's wife
- Thrown into jail

All this before he was redeemed, reunited with his family, made one of the most powerful men in Egypt, and credited with ensuring the survival of Egypt (Gen. 37-45).

The Path Is Rarely a Straight One

While my story isn't as eventful as Joseph's, over my decades in business and beyond, I've become very familiar with feeling like I was lost and on the wrong path. In fact, I didn't start thinking I had begun to hit my stride and move into my purpose until my 30s. Even now, I continue to refine my vision as new opportunities present themselves.

In college, my major was special education, with a minor in elementary education. Unfortunately, the second I was in front of a class of students, I knew I didn't belong there. Still, I stuck it out for three years, knowing I was in the wrong place but not knowing what was next. I thought maybe a graduate degree would allow me to get out of the classroom but still make use of my training and my leadership skills, so I got a master's degree in administration and supervision.

I liked it a bit better, but I still felt the mismatch deep inside. So if a master's degree wasn't the ticket to fulfillment, surely a PhD would help, right? I was well into my doctorate when I got a call that would change my life. I was approached by a manager who was recruiting for a well-known insurance company, and he had come across my resume. He had a business opportunity. Would I be interested in talking?

Would I? Definitely. I would have talked to *anybody* at that point. When I met with him and heard about the opportunity, I said, "This is what I'm looking for! I can be my own boss, create my own business ... I'm in." That jump from education took me in a brand-new direction, but even then, all was not perfect. In fact, I thought I'd made a huge mistake at first because I dreaded cold-calling leads, wasn't used to being rejected, and had a different style than my training manager.

It took some time before I got the freedom I had craved and realized, "This is what I was meant to do." It didn't become easier — I was still getting rejected and was still facing a huge learning curve — but my business was *mine*. I was able to utilize the skills, expertise, and instincts I possessed, and that allowed me to flourish as an agent and become one of the top 100 in the country that first year.

That was just the beginning, though. I'd be faced with more change, more opportunities, more learning, and more failure ... but it was all part of the process of becoming who I knew I was meant to be, doing the work I knew I was meant to do.

I tell you this story to show you that first, you're never too old to find your path. If you don't feel like you know what you're here for yet, don't despair — there's plenty of time. Second, I want you to embrace the idea that your mission is ever-evolving, one that is more of a process than a distinct goal. The clues are there, and like a treasure hunt, each of us has to do the legwork to get closer and closer to the goal of living in line with our purpose.

Embrace the Journey

If you've achieved a level of success in your career, you're a get-it-done person. You probably have to-do lists, annual plans, and systems for keeping things on track as you pursue your personal, professional, and organizational goals. That ability to analyze and execute efficiently and effectively has served you well as a leader.

But what do you do when the end goal isn't quite so clear? "Living a bold mission" can cover a lot of ground, and there's no one-size-fits-all approach — a reality that can be really difficult for driven, high-achieving individuals to accept. We like certainty and direction, complete with timelines and status reports.

One of the hardest things about identifying and living into your mission is that it can seem like the majority of the time is spent wandering around, experimenting, and taking one small step at a time. Efficiency and productivity often have to be set aside in favor of exploration and curiosity. You may have to make what looks like false starts before you end up where you're supposed to be. As someone who prides herself on progress, it was very hard for me to feel like I was wasting time or that I had made some huge mistake because I knew I was in the wrong role. There are always lessons to be learned in whatever space you're in. There's no better example of this than my friend and client Martha.

Rising from the Ashes

Martha was born in dirt-floor poverty in Mexico and came to Phoenix with her mother when she was only 11. "For the first time, we had hot and cold water," she recalls. "You could just turn it on and off!" She wasn't very interested in schooling and ended up dropping out of high school before graduation and hooking up with one of the flashy, older guys she'd seen around town. She knew he was into some shady activities, including drug dealing, but she wasn't aware that she was living with the devil, she says.

Flash forward through years of physical and mental abuse, the birth of two boys, and almost total isolation from her friends and family. Only 22, she knew she had to get away from her abuser, even if it meant losing her life trying.

She almost did lose her life when her boyfriend started attacking her, and she pulled a gun on him. In the ensuing struggle, he grabbed the gun from her and shot her point-blank in front of her children. Inexplicably, he looked down at her as she lay bleeding, then turned around and left her there. The next thing she knew, she woke up in the hospital, ecstatic because she and her children were free.

But then reality set in. She was a single mom with no education and no skills — how was she going to support her two little boys? Her mother, who worked for a janitorial company, had the answer. "You know how to clean a toilet," she said. "Come work with me."

And so Martha did. As small as it was, the first $300 paycheck she held in her hands was a sign of her strength. She threw herself into her work, learning everything about the business … and within a matter of years, she started her own janitorial company. Over the next 20 years, she'd add three more businesses to the mix. One of her guiding principles is helping her employees become self-sufficient and eventually start their own businesses.

Did Martha know when she started cleaning offices that she would eventually employ hundreds of people and help them better their own lives? That she would meet with the Mexican embassy to talk about cross-cultural entrepreneurial programs? Or that she'd be awarded the 2021 Champion of Freedom medal? No. But each step of the way on her path, she was committed to learning, doing her best, and growing into the next opportunity.

Her mission is to help others to fly and reach their own dreams. How she accomplishes that will continue to change and evolve as she takes on new challenges.

The Clues to Your Mission

Are you tempted to think there is no major theme connecting all your experiences? Most of us feel this way at some point, but it's only in reflection and in the rearview mirror that all the pieces begin to fit together in a pattern. Just like Martha, me or any of the other people in this book, finding your purpose will be a process of refining, exploring, testing, and trying.

That being said, there are some clues I've found that I use to work with my clients when they're narrowing in on their unique life purpose. Use these as you review your life and career for patterns and indications of your next steps.

Clue #1: It benefits others. This is pretty obvious, but it bears mentioning. I have yet to see a person with a life purpose that is completely self-focused. For each bold mission,there is always an element of philanthropy, outreach, or societal impact. That doesn't mean you have to sell all you own and devote yourself to rescuing sea turtles. It might, but it also might mean you create a med spa, like my friend Carol, where your clients feel pampered in their bodies, hearts, and souls.

Carol tells her staff that it may look like they're working in a med spa, but it's actually a mission! She has story after story of women and men she's helped with some of life's most challenging and heartbreaking occurrences, from death to illness to loneliness. She is a successful businessperson. But more than that, she's on a mission to serve others.

Clue #2: You're doing things you love that are in line with what you're good at ... When you're headed in the right direction, there's something deep inside you that lights up. It's an inner peace that can be difficult to fully articulate, like your soul is standing up and saying, "YES!"

When I started my insurance business, I knew the learning curve was steep, but I also immediately felt that I was where I was supposed to be — as opposed to the lack of fulfillment I felt in front of the classroom! How I felt in those two circumstances was completely different, like wearing a pair of shoes a size too small and then slipping into the ones made just for you.

Clue #3: … AND you'll be asked to grow. At the same time you'll feel like you're in your element, being a purpose-driven leader will also require you to learn new skills, improve existing strengths, and adapt to changing situations. You'll need courage, resilience, and strength to walk your path. You will be called on to grow and evolve as a leader and person, and you may feel you're not up to the task. But if you are called to something, you will be equipped to do so. As the Bible says, "I can do all things through Christ who strengthens me" (Phil. 4:13, NKJV).

A sentiment attributed to Aristotle sums up the idea of finding your purpose: "Where your talents and the world's needs cross, there lies your vocation." Look for that intersection, and you'll be on the right track.

PART ONE WRAP-UP

As we wrap up this section on BELIEVE, the main takeaway I want to leave you with is this: The world needs you and your mission. You matter, and your dreams and goals matter — not just to you but to the people around you as well. There is a special role for you to play in building God's kingdom on earth. Through your previous experiences, skills, and strengths, you probably already have at least a hint of what that role is and where you're meant to journey next. Now you need to believe you are called to claim your leadership even more boldly than you have.

If you look at your life and are wondering if there's a way to make sense of this odd assortment of where you've been, what you've learned, and what is still inside of you, the answer is YES. Everything you've done so far has brought you to this point. It is not a coincidence that you are reading these words and are feeling the pull to live a more meaningful life.

Before we move forward into the next section on OWNING your mission, take time to absorb this truth in your heart: God created you for this time and this place. Believe it!

> *"For I know the plans I have for you," declares the Lord, "plans to prosper you and not to harm you, plans to give you hope and a future."*
>
> –Jer. 29:11, NIV

OWN IT

Have you ever known something to be unquestionably, undoubtedly true, yet you still lived your life as if that knowledge was optional?

Whether it's knowing you've outgrown your current position, knowing that a new hire just isn't going to work out, or knowing that a relationship or friendship is no longer serving you ... You still continue on.

Then there are other times when you wake up — sometimes literally in the middle of the night — with a realization that is so unavoidable that you can never go back. Your actions will have to align with your knowledge because you can no longer live out of alignment with what you know to be true. It's now nonnegotiable.

That is the difference between believing and owning your calling.

Owning your calling is what makes some people abruptly quit school, buy the ticket to Paris, or push "print" on their letter of resignation. These "Aha!" moments are what books and movies are made of. *Jerry Maguire, Star Wars, Spider-Man* ... they all are examples of the main character being faced with knowledge they can no longer put on the back burner or ignore.

Most people, even those who are ready to own their mission, don't make an instantaneous U-turn. It's more typically a process of continuous, gradual movement, of putting one step after the other. While huge, immediate shifts are great for drama, real life typically requires more preparation and forethought. And while we love to read about and watch people upend their lives, it's rarely realistic or advisable to make rash decisions in our own lives.

When I work with my clients, I see that owning their dreams — even big, bold ones — is more a series of consistent decisions rather than an abrupt earthquake. I'm a big advocate for research and planning and taking calculated steps rather than simply plugging your nose and jumping in the deep end. Moving deliberately and intentionally forward allows you to make better decisions, foresee challenges and obstacles (of which there will be plenty), and incorporate support from others.

A more considered pace also lets you deal with one of the biggest challenges of all: fear.

One of the biggest myths about leadership is that you'll someday reach a point where you no longer feel fear. In my experience — and in the experiences of the thousands of people

I've worked with over the years — that point will never come. As long as you are pushing forward and growing, you will continue to move outside your comfort zone, and you will continue to doubt your ability to succeed. You'll still be frightened; you'll just be much better at dealing with it and limiting its effects on your life.

Over the course of my career, I've felt unprepared for just about every promotion I received. I would wonder, "Can I do this? What if I'm not equipped? I'm not sure I'm ready." Even the writing of this book caused more than a few moments of uncertainty and doubt. Because I believed so strongly in my vision, though, I kept moving forward despite my anxiety. While the fear never fully dissipates, the more you push back against it, the weaker its ability to control your thoughts and actions becomes.

I'll share more stories in the upcoming chapters about people who felt the fear and did it anyway. People who had all the excuses in the world not to push themselves but felt they had to because the cost of *not* acting was just too great. People who believed they had a bold purpose in life and then owned that knowledge. People who knew deep inside that the future ahead held rewards and gifts that were worth fighting for. People like you.

My goal in this section is to help you anticipate the challenges ahead and start preparing for them now. The path to impact is never an easy one, but it is one you can successfully navigate. You'll know you're fully owning your purpose when your decisions come from a place of strength and courage rather than fear and worry.

I love this passage from the book of Isaiah in the Old Testament.

> *So do not fear, for I am with you; do not be dismayed, for I am your God. I will strengthen you and help you; I will uphold you with my righteous right hand.*
>
> —Isa. 41:10, NIV

Own this truth: When you are driven by your desire to serve others and to serve God, you will never be alone.

Chapter 5

Excuses, Excuses

I magine this scenario: Your phone rings. It's your boss who says that the speaker for the company's national sales meeting had to cancel at the last minute. Are you available to step in? Oh, by the way, the meeting is in Hawaii, and you can have a few days of vacation right after. The only catch is that the presentation is tomorrow, and you have to fly out right away.

What's your natural response? Do you grab your laptop and swimsuit and head to the airport, or do you immediately come up with a million-and-one reasons why you couldn't possibly honor such a last-minute request? *"Well, I have a team meeting on Thursday, and I really don't know what I would talk about, so I think I'll pass."*

The truth is, most people would rather miss what could be the opportunity of a lifetime rather than take a step into the unknown. Humans are creatures of habit, and anything that threatens our routine is viewed with suspicion rather than excitement. We justify our resistance to change with a long list of reasonable-sounding excuses.

In fact, one of the definitions of excuse is "justification, reason."[5] And while our reasons for inaction might sound legitimate, they're really just explanations we give ourselves for staying right where we are, avoiding risk, and playing small.

This desire to stay in our comfort zones is one reason why so few people actually pursue their big dreams. There are just so many reasons not to do so! As soon as someone begins toying with the idea of taking a risk or stepping outside their comfort zone, the excuses pop up. "I'm too old …" "I don't know where to start …" "I'm so busy right now …" and on and on. And the bigger the dream, the longer the list of excuses.

The Four Excuse Traps

In my experience, excuses that may arise for you as you contemplate your mission will fall into four main categories:

- **Finances.** It's common to ask, "Will I be able to make money following my passion?" or to say, "I can't afford to start a company/go back to school/etc." I don't want to downplay this very real concern because money is a reality of life and one that can cause issues. But finances also can be a convenient excuse that cloaks other worries. After all, if you say, "Oh, I couldn't take that new job because it would have affected my family's finances," everyone would understand and think you were just being responsible. But please make sure you're being honest with yourself. Is money really a big problem, or are you trying to avoid taking action because of unfounded fears about not being able to support yourself or your family? I believe that if God is calling you to something, he will support you through that process. Philippians 4:19 (NIV) says, "And my God will meet all your needs according to the riches of his glory in Christ Jesus."

- **Age.** I've heard people say, "I'm too old to start XYZ." I've also heard people say, "I'm too young to start XYZ." This seems to be the one-size-fits-all excuse, with one person saying they're too old to change jobs/write a book/start over in a new city, while someone else is saying they're too young to do the identical thing! Hint: There is no magic age (or age limit) for following your dreams. There are both those older and younger than you who have done the very thing you long to do. Biblically, Abraham and Sara were well into their old age when their son Isaac, one of the patriarchs of the Jewish people, was born. Meanwhile, David, the future King of Israel, was only a teenager when he killed the giant Goliath and saved the Israelites.

- **Experience.** This is a very common excuse, and it's often true — which is why it can be so dangerous. When you are moving toward your purpose, you'll be called on, again and again, to enter new realms and learn new skills. If you try to resist your vision because you've never started a nonprofit, run for office, spoken in front of a large group, or asked others to support your efforts in some way, there's just one thing I want to say: There's a first time for everything. Throughout my own career, I have been asked to step up and accept roles that initially seemed beyond my abilities. Yes, there were times when I was intimidated … but I had my "cheering squad" reminding me that my leadership team chose ME for the role. When I relied on my instinct, skills, and the experience I did have, I was able to grow into the position and demonstrate my expertise. (We'll be talking more about how you can develop your own support network in chapter 10, so stay tuned.)

- **Risk.** Some people acknowledge and believe their dreams, but then they pass them off, saying, "Well, I'm just not the type of person who would do that." What they mean is that up until this point, they haven't been the type of person to take risks or move boldly in a new direction. The key is that this may have been true *until this point*, but things can and do change. Our lives don't always continue on the same track, and you are now being called to something bigger and more meaningful. Going away to college, starting your first job, and expanding your responsibilities all required you to step out in faith. Think of this as just another in a long line of growth opportunities that will occur throughout your life.

After reading through these four categories, which excuses have come up for you? You may want to write down the ones that come up most often. Think about what is really true and what may simply be your mind's attempt to keep you safe. Remember, just because you think or feel something doesn't mean it's true. And even if it's been true up until now, it doesn't mean it must be true forever.

Feel the Fear and Do It Anyway

If you haven't figured it out already, excuses are a less vulnerable way of saying, "I'm scared." It's much more acceptable to tell your boss, "Thank you for the invitation, but I simply have too much on my plate," than to say, "Are you kidding? The last time I tried to speak in front of a group, I threw up and tripped over my feet on my way to the stage. No thank you!" But both amount to the same thing: a way of avoiding venturing into the unknown.

When I coach people who are at an earlier point in their careers, they are often surprised when I assure them that even the most accomplished executives in their companies, at times, feel anxiety, worry, and fear. In fact, I've never met anyone — from politicians to multimillion-dollar entrepreneurs to leaders in the armed forces — who doesn't sometimes feel intimidated or downright scared. The question is not, "When will I stop feeling fear?" Instead, it's, "When will I stop letting fear stop me?" How you handle fear is what makes all the difference in who you become and what kind of leader you can be.

Being courageous doesn't mean not feeling fear. It means feeling the fear and then taking action despite your emotions.

There was one time in my career when I was asked to head up a statewide professional women's association with a membership base of over 20,000. At the same time, I was taking on a larger role in my company and leading a team that needed new direction. Both positions required a lot of me — consensus-building, strong leadership, and making tough decisions that I'd have to sell to the rest of the organization. I was so uncertain about my ability to perform that I retreated into myself, becoming a smaller, less confident version of who I knew myself to be. I thought I was playing it safe by keeping a low profile, but instead, I was undercutting my own ability to lead.

After one board meeting, where I bit my tongue and hid my opinions, one of my mentors, Cindy, followed me out. "Who was that in that meeting?" she demanded. "That wasn't you!"

Immediately, the lightbulb went off. I was acting a different way — overly accommodating, soft, and quiet — because I was hesitant to embrace my confidence, instincts, and knowledge and lead the way I knew I needed to. Both on the board and in the office, I was trying to be who I thought people wanted me to be, not who I knew I *needed* to be to move things forward. Both organizations needed bold leadership, and I was giving them mush.

When I stepped into the role and owned it, I was able to make effective change, bring people together, and actually lead in my own style. I didn't need to change myself to fit in or please others out of fear; I needed to show up — confident and courageous — and act from there, even if I felt scared doing it!

Role Models for Courage

If there's anyone who should have excuses for trying to play it safe, it's my client Lisa. She experienced a childhood full of trauma and abuse that is something right out of a horror novel. At age 16, Lisa finally left home, despite her misgivings and fear about her own self-worth, her value to others, and her ability to simply survive.

If that was all she'd done in her life, I would say that she had risen above her circumstances and made a success of herself. But Lisa's story doesn't stop there. She joined the U.S. Army, became a helicopter mechanic, and because of her mental strength and leadership, was promoted to crew chief. Again, if the story stopped there, it would be amazing ... but there's more.

After being medically discharged from the Army when a serious accident left her unable to perform her duties, Lisa started thinking about her next chapter in life. She'd always loved numbers and data, so she thought accounting would be a great field. Despite being a single mother of two, she got her degree and passed the very rigorous CPA exam. Today, she is a partner in one of the oldest, most well-respected accounting firms in her state.

Did she feel fear along the way? Of course. But she knew that she was meant for more. She had goals and dreams, and the visions of what could be drowned out the voices telling her that she couldn't do it, that she was worthless, and that she would fail. The excuses, the worry, the negative voices ... Lisa heard them and then kept moving forward anyway. Now she's on another mission, this time to create her own boutique agency.

Making the Choice for More

As you think about what owning your mission or purpose means for you, don't let the excuses, fears, or worries discourage you. Find role models like Lisa in your own life. Look for people who have overcome the odds and faced challenges you could only imagine. There are many of them in this book, and they're probably all around you, too. Let them inspire you. And while you're at it, keep a running list of the challenges you yourself have overcome.

Maybe you had a less-than-ideal childhood. Maybe you grew up in poverty. Maybe you have struggled with dyslexia or another perceived limitation. Think about all the ways you've already faced your fears and come out the other side stronger and more capable.

I don't want to make it sound like living boldly is easy because often it is not. Sometimes it seems like the distance between you and your dreams gets bigger every day and as soon as you solve one problem, another arises to take its place. You are trading comfort for something much more rewarding (we'll talk about tradeoffs in the next chapter).

Fear won't ever disappear entirely, but your skills and confidence can and will increase to meet it. Whether you're facing fear of failure, fear of rejection, or fear of discomfort, if you are called to something greater, you will find a way. When you doubt your abilities, remember the words of the Apostle Paul in the New Testament:

> I can do all things through Christ who strengthens me ... And my God shall supply all your needs according to His riches in glory by Christ Jesus.
> –Phil. 4:13, 19, NKJV

Chapter 6

What Is Your Mission Worth to You?

Choosing to own a bold calling in your life will require sacrifices and trade-offs. You're making a choice to move outside your comfort zone with no guarantees about what will happen as a result. You'll give up what you know in order to embrace the unknown, and you may need to let go of parts of your current life in order to accept something new. That process of trading *what is* for *what could be* can be a difficult one.

No one knows this better than my cousin Gina. She is a perfect example of having every reason to say "no" to accepting a new, bigger life assignment — but saying "yes" anyway because something inside her wouldn't let her settle for where she was.

Gina had a degree in psychology but stayed home with her two sets of twins, including one son with cerebral palsy. When he was born more than 20 years ago, she was overwhelmed by what his diagnosis would mean for her and her family and how they would navigate a lifetime of care and financial sacrifice.

As her young family grew, she devoted herself wholeheartedly to her role as a mother. But then, something new started to take root and grow within her. She felt she was being called to become a licensed counselor — a process that is intense for anyone, let alone a 40-something mom of four with a disabled child.

From the outside, taking on another commitment made no sense. Who would take care of all the household responsibilities while she was in school and then in training? How would the family function without her constant presence? What about finances? Gina and her husband wrestled with all these questions. Yet she simply couldn't ignore the messages she was receiving from God, and so she moved forward.

Now, Gina is a licensed professional counselor and relationship expert. She uses her unique experiences with grief and family challenges to help private clients and groups be more successful in their own lives. Her sacrifices of time, energy, and money have paid off in a thriving practice — all because she was willing to let go of the life she had in order to move into something larger, something she felt she was meant to do.

As you look at your own calling, I don't want you to ignore the trade-offs you will need to make because they are real. Instead, I want you to evaluate them with an open mind, looking at both what you may lose and what you may gain. Gina decided that despite the sacrifices, saying "no" came at too high a cost. What is the risk of saying "no" to your dream?

No Safe Spaces

As we discussed previously, life is not all sunshine and roses when you say "yes" to your dreams. You will face challenges. You will face rejection. You will face failure. All of this can be painful. But staying where you are isn't guaranteed to be safe, either.

In fact, staying where you are may be the riskiest thing of all. Many of us feel like we shouldn't want more because our life right now is pretty good, and we don't want to rock the boat. That feeling is very common — and natural.

While I don't seek out risk, I also don't shy away from it. In my corporate career, I moved 11 times in order to take different roles within the company. Each and every time, I made that decision carefully. I discussed it with my husband. I prayed about it. I analyzed it from different angles. I was clear on the personal and professional sacrifices of both saying "yes" AND saying "no" because there is always a trade-off with any choice.

Because we said "yes" to growth and advancement, Ed and I said goodbye to friends, church communities, and cities that we loved. We sold furniture and houses, traded wardrobes from one climate to another, and we moved forward into the unknown in a very literal sense as we started over time after time. These sacrifices weren't in vain. We made new friends. We explored new towns. We had experiences we never would have, had we stayed in one place. I grew as a leader and as a person. Our commitment to each other and to our faith matured. It was rarely easy, but the risks were worth what we received in return.

Taking Stock

As someone who is successful in your own life, you probably also have a decision-making process that involves weighing the pros and cons. Whether you're deciding to hire a new employee or choosing between two locations for your next vacation, you likely go through a cost-benefit analysis. When I work with my clients, I suggest they go through a similar exercise when they're wrestling with their dreams.

One tendency I see is to look only at the downside of taking a risk. You might focus on the cost of going back to school or the fallout if you run for office and your neighbors or coworkers disagree with your positions. Yes, there are very real risks involved, but every choice has pluses *and* minuses. Instead of looking at just one side of the equation, you need to look at the whole picture. What do you get if you stay where you are? What might you lose? Now, look at what you will risk if you move forward. What will you receive?

When I think of weighing risks and rewards, Dr. Michael Miller comes to mind. A talented plastic surgeon, throughout his career, he opposed performing gender reassignment surgery for transgendered individuals despite growing pressure from colleagues to change his views. His opposition led to costly personal and professional consequences. He became increasingly marginalized until it became necessary to step down from a highly respected leadership position in academic medicine. Still, losing his integrity was never worth the short-lived and hollow benefits of yielding to the pressure. He now strives to be a voice for reason and freedom for many others in the medical profession.

When you say yes to a larger dream for your life, you may be facing risks:

1. Personal risks (finances, time, discomfort, the unknown)
2. Professional risks (failure, rejection)
3. Societal risks (rejection from others, going against the popular narrative, being "canceled")

On the other hand, there is also much to be gained by moving forward in faith:

1. Personal rewards (financial reward, excitement, fulfillment, peace)
2. Professional rewards (professional accolades and growth, advancement)
3. Societal rewards (new relationships, new opportunities)

You might find this chart useful to make sure you're evaluating all aspects of your decision:

Stay Where I Am	Venture Forward
Risks: • Personal • Professional • Societal	Risks: • Personal • Professional • Societal
Rewards: • Personal • Professional • Societal	Rewards: • Personal • Professional • Societal

Is Enough, Enough?

One thought that may come up as you go through your analysis is the idea of having "enough." I hear this concept from people a lot. They say, "I am not sure I should risk what I have for something more when I have enough. Am I being greedy? Should I just be satisfied where I am right now?"

Many people, particularly women, feel it's somehow wrong to want more — more fulfillment, more purpose, more friends, more growth, more meaning, and even more money. We wonder, *Who are we to ask for something else when we've been blessed with so much?* Or, like Gina, you might wonder if the impact on your family is worth pursuing your dreams.

This question makes me think of this Bible verse from the book of Luke in the New Testament:

> *From everyone who has been given much, much will be demanded; and from the one who has been entrusted with much, much more will be asked.*
> –Luke 12:48, NIV

As a Christian, I believe we are here not for ourselves but to build up others. We are not here for a life of comfort and ease but a life of growth and meaning. If we have blessings, it's for the purpose of sharing them with others, even when it requires us to leave our comfort zone and take risks.

The verse from Luke goes hand-in-hand with one of Jesus' most famous parables, the parable of the talents. In this teaching story found in the book of Matthew, a man is leaving town for an extended period of time. He calls three of his servants to him and gives them each a sum of money, called a talent.

The first two servants took the money, did some smart business deals, and doubled their money. The third servant, though, was worried about losing his master's property, so he took the money and buried it in the ground.

When the master returned home, he checked in with his team. Seeing what the first two servants had done, he was pleased and gave them even more money to invest, saying, "Well done, good and faithful servant. You have been faithful over a little; I will set you over much" (Matt. 25:21, ESV). But when the third servant shared the news that he hadn't done anything with the money he'd been trusted with, the master was angry because he had wasted the opportunity to do good.

The master takes the money away, gives it to the first servant, and throws the third servant out of the household, saying, "For to everyone who has will more be given, and he will have an abundance. But from the one who has not, even what he has will be taken away" (Matt. 25:29, ESV).

We are given gifts not to hoard them, squander them, or guard them but to use them to create more truth, love, generosity, and kindness in the world for the benefit of others. If you look at your life and see a wealth of blessings, good friends, financial security, and joy, be grateful. You're not selfish for wanting more; you're selfish if you don't try to use what you have to help those who have not been so blessed. When we have "enough" for ourselves, our job is now to increase that so we can share it with others.

The Most Important Question of All

As you can see, performing a logical analysis of your choices using the table above is useful. But it's only one tool to use when choosing whether or not to accept and embrace your mission. Not all risks are equal, and not all rewards are assured.

In my own life and while coaching my clients, I ask one question that can override just about everything else. It's only five words, but it's incredibly powerful. The question is, "Am I capable of more?"

This question is direct and to the point. It cuts through much of the confusion and fear that can accompany thinking outside your current circumstance. It demands that you answer honestly, with a simple yes or no. Either there is more you can learn, more good you can do, and more people you can help, or there is not. Either you are at the pinnacle of your achievement right now, or there is still more in you and more for you to do.

The Bible is full of people called out of their "ordinary" into something grander: Moses, Noah, Abraham and Sara, Joseph, Queen Esther, Jonah, King David, Mary, Jesus' twelve apostles... They all had to leave behind one life in order to help their communities, their families, and God's people as a whole. If you're not acquainted with these stories, I encourage you to research them and see how they were called to leave the familiar behind in order to fill important roles in human history. Just like my cousin Gina, each one of them could easily have said, "I'm good. I don't need to do more." But instead, they realized that saying "no" wasn't an option. There was a greater assignment for them to accomplish, one that they couldn't turn their back on. If they did, they'd be faced with a life of regret, wondering what might have been.

That's the real conundrum you must wrestle with. What if you were created for a specific purpose (you were!), and you were hesitant to accept it? You must decide which is worse, saying "no" and remaining where you are, or saying "yes" and potentially failing.

I'm in favor of taking calculated risks, and one way of minimizing the negative results of any decision is to thoroughly prepare yourself for the journey ahead. In the next chapter, we'll talk about how to prepare yourself for the challenges you will face as you pursue your mission. I'll close this chapter with one of my favorite verses:

> *And we know that in all things God works for the good of those who love him, who have been called according to his purpose.*
>
> –Rom. 8:28, NIV

When you own your calling, it will lead to a more authentic expression of yourself and who you were created to be.

Chapter 7

Preparing for the Journey

Let's revisit that surprise work trip to Hawaii that I mentioned earlier. If you said "yes" to the opportunity, what's the first thing you'd do before you embark on the journey? Most likely, you'd ask for details about the presentation, get a copy of the itinerary, and then pack your bags as you prepare for your trip.

Knowing you're headed to Hawaii is important because your destination drives all other decisions, but your preparation doesn't stop there. How long is your presentation? Do you need your own A/V setup, or is one provided? How large will the audience be? How long will you be gone? What events will you attend? Do you need cash, or will credit cards work? What island are you going to? Where will you stay? Do you need to arrange transportation to the hotel? There's a long list of details to consider, but the more prework you do, the easier the trip will be.

Preparation for your mission is critical, too. That includes reviewing your resources, researching what you'll need for the journey and the destination, and identifying the gaps in your knowledge and resources.

Even when you're passionate about your calling, it's essential to look ahead and plan your route. Passion will take you far, but it won't replace proper preparation. While you won't be able to anticipate every step of the path, laying out the pieces you do know will make the journey smoother.

When I think about preparing for a journey, the story of the Israelites escaping Egypt in the book of Exodus comes to mind. What should have been an 11-day journey ended up taking 40 years! While that was largely because of the Israelites' disobedience rather than lack of preparation, I still remind myself that thoughtful planning can prevent a lot of wasted time and energy.

Counting the costs of our projects before we start is wise. In the book of Luke, Jesus asks,

> *For which of you, desiring to build a tower, does not first sit down and count the cost, whether he has enough to complete it? Otherwise, when he has laid a foundation and is not able to finish, all who see it begin to mock him, saying, 'This man began to build and was not able to finish.'*
> –Luke 14:28-30, ESV

Counting the Cost

Whether you want to launch a new business, write a book, go back to school, or embark on pretty much any other big goal, there will be financial costs involved — often more than you anticipate. You may be foregoing a higher salary while you start your new venture. You may need to hire a team to help you. You may need to design a logo, get a website designed, purchase supplies, invest in training ... The list goes on.

My advice is to start with what you know, put a cost range on it, and add some padding. It's much better to estimate too high a cost and have a surplus than estimate too low and end up scrambling to make up the difference.

In addition to funds, there are other areas you'll want to assess, including:

- **Skills.** We talked a lot about what skills and talents you already possess in chapter 3. Now, what additional skills will you need to accomplish your goal? Many of my clients need to polish their interpersonal skills. Others want to upgrade their personal appearance. How are you at motivating and leading others? What about time management?

    My friend Ericka was already a skilled manicurist, but when she decided to start her own salon, she needed to be able to manage others effectively. In order for my client Nathan to spread the word about his medical knowledge, he needed to be a powerful public speaker, so I've been coaching him on that skill. What skills do you need to strengthen?

- **Resources.** Finances are, of course, a big concern. When I first started my own insurance agency, I cashed out my teacher retirement in order to invest in my business. Resources go beyond finances. Think about what kind of time you'll need to invest in your project — is there a gap between your available time and the hours needed? If so, where can you make up the difference? Gina, whom you met in chapter 6, knew her schooling and training would require long hours, so she and her husband made a plan for how they'd cover the times she needed to be in class or at her internship. Can you hire help or ask others to come alongside you?

  And speaking of asking others, when it comes to assessing your resources, don't overlook your network. People are a resource, potentially the most valuable one of all. Who do you know who can provide assistance and input?

- **Knowledge and expertise.** Knowledge and expertise refer to specialized topic areas that go beyond skill.

For instance, running for political office requires a lot of specialized knowledge to ensure you're staying on the right side of the myriad rules and regulations regarding financing, getting on the ballot, and running your campaign. Likewise, starting a business or nonprofit will probably mean getting legal advice at some point.

Just in writing this book, I've worked with an editor, photographer, designer, writer, and publisher ... all of whom possess competencies in areas far beyond my expertise!

Don't get discouraged because you don't know what you don't know; instead, make a list of what you need, and call in the experts. That's exactly what my friend Michelle Moore did when she decided to start a nonprofit to aid mothers in crisis.

A Touch of Grace

If there's a woman who knows how to get things done, it's Michelle Moore. Michelle is a mom of three, a senior VP with a healthcare diagnostics company, and the founder of Mother's Grace, a charity aimed at helping mothers through the toughest times in their lives.

Michelle lost her mom at age 5. While she was dealing with breast cancer and in the hospital recovering from a double mastectomy, her young son was diagnosed with type 1 diabetes. At that time, she wanted nothing more than to have her own mom there to comfort and help her. Never one to focus on her own struggles, she decided to create a nonprofit to help other mothers experiencing crises like the loss of a child, illness, or other trauma. There was just one problem; she had no idea how to start a nonprofit!

Michelle wasn't going to let her lack of knowledge stop her, so she started making phone calls. She reached out to anyone she thought might be able to help, from the First Lady of Arizona to an attorney and an accountant. Now, the Mother's Grace board includes people with distinct skills and experience, all of whom are ready to step up to meet the challenges of running a 100-percent volunteer charity.

To date, Mother's Grace has helped over 3,000 families in Arizona (and more around the world) and has granted over $5 million to families in need, all because Michelle saw a need and stepped forward to meet it, despite not knowing how she was going to make it all work.

I love Michelle's story because it demonstrates a lot of the principles that are needed for bold leaders: curiosity, humility, creativity, and a willingness to move forward even when you can't see the whole path ahead of you. Michelle never looked for a road map; she just kept taking one step after another, adjusting along the way.

One Small Step

One of the most exciting — and anxiety-producing — aspects of owning your dream is that it's impossible to know exactly what it will look like. As Michelle demonstrated, you may have an idea of what you want to create, but you're a bit fuzzy on the specifics. Don't let that stop you. All the people in this book will tell you that they began with a broad vision of what they felt called to do, and only through the process did they begin to narrow in on the details.

My cousin Gina had an idea she wanted to be a counselor, but she wasn't clear about what that meant until she researched the profession's requirements. As she got further into her training and began to establish her own practice, she naturally fell into an expertise that fit her perfectly.

After she left the Army, Lisa, whom you met in chapter 5, knew she wanted to explore her love of and skill with numbers and quantitative analysis, but she wasn't sure what that would look like. She researched different careers, gained clarity about what she enjoyed and what skills she already had, and then made the decision to pursue her CPA license.

Michelle wanted to help moms in crisis feel less alone. Her first efforts involved getting together with a handful of girlfriends and raising a few thousand dollars to help mothers in crisis with gift cards, gasoline, and other essentials. She had no idea then that within a few years, she'd have a full-fledged

501(c) charity that would grant millions of dollars to families in need. She would never have seen the "promised land" if she hadn't taken that first step … and then the next … and then the next.

So how do you know what that first step is? You ask.

Ask and You Shall Receive

Talking with someone who has done what you want to do can provide unrivaled insight and guidance. Whether you want to start a cosmetics company or build a school in a developing country, someone out there has accomplished something close to what you dream of. Track them down, and ask questions! Most people are very willing to share their experiences, particularly when they sense the passion behind your interest.

Don't know who to talk to? Get creative. Ask everyone you know if they know someone who has done the thing you want to do. Read books and listen to podcasts and then contact the featured expert. Find people on LinkedIn. Remember, this is your dream — don't let the fact that you don't yet know a person dissuade you from reaching out to them! Ask for 15 minutes of their time, and go from there.

The Bible says, "Plans fail for lack of counsel, but with many advisers they succeed" (Prov. 15:22, NIV).

Here's a starter list of questions to ask your advisers or experts:

Informational Interview Questions

- Where did you get the idea for XYZ?
- What were the biggest barriers you faced?
- How did you handle them?
- Who helped you along the way?
- What happened that you didn't expect?
- What do you wish you'd done differently?
- Who else should I speak with?
- May I contact you again if I have additional questions, or just to let you know how it's going?

A word about trying to do things on your own: It doesn't work. Michelle knew she needed many hands in order to reach more women who needed help to get through the worst times in their lives. She didn't try to become an expert in fundraising, accounting, law, and event planning. She partnered with people. She set her ego aside in service of the goal of helping women in crisis.

Talking with other people helps you fill in the gaps in what you're doing and also helps allay your fears. Talking to just one person who has successfully launched their own bakery or adopted a child from foster care shows it can be done. Fears evaporate when exposed to hope, and that's exactly what these conversations will give you. You'll also realize no one is completely ready for their bold future!

As you gather more information, take notes. Make lists of what you know and what you don't know. Follow the breadcrumbs as they lead you from one person to the next or one resource to the next. You'll begin to see where the pieces start to fit together, where God is guiding you, and where you need to move next.

Another amazing thing is that as you start researching, the picture becomes more clear, and your fear will start to abate. The huge journey becomes just one step at a time.

PART TWO WRAP-UP

As you can see, OWNING your mission requires not just a mental shift but a shift in commitment as well. At this stage, your dream is no longer just a partially formed idea but an actual goal you will devote time, money, and other resources toward achieving.

When you take this next step, don't be surprised when things seem to take on a life of their own! You may meet someone who becomes the perfect advisor. Or a friend might send you a link to a podcast episode with the exact encouragement you need. These aren't random occurrences. These serendipitous moments are sent from God to confirm you're on the right path.

You also may start to feel fear and doubt. Though anxiety is natural, you don't have to listen to the voices (inside or outside of your head) that tell you that you're being foolish or taking unnecessary risks. Remember, living boldly requires a trade-off. Check in with yourself and your "why," and ask yourself if the risk is worth the reward, both for you and for those around you.

If you have something in you that can make this world a better place, don't delay. You owe it to yourself and to those who will be impacted by your work to embrace your calling. The time is now!

As long as it is day, we must do the works of him who sent me. Night is coming, when no one can work.
–John 9:4, NIV

LIVE IT

A s we discussed in the previous section, planning is essential to any goal or mission. It is common sense that you shouldn't embark on a project without first doing an analysis of costs and potential pitfalls and before identifying a proposed path. Research is a critical first phase of successful execution.

But planning or thinking about your mission is not living it, any more than planning a vacation is the same as taking one. Bringing your dream out of the idea phase and into action is where things get real. There comes a point where you have to lease the building, hire the staff, buy the plane ticket, or turn in the letter of resignation ... That's when things take off! Until that point, the whole process of exploring even the biggest dream is still fairly safe. You haven't actually risked anything except some dream time and mental effort. But living your mission requires you to move out of the planning, researching, and dreaming stage and into actual decision-making and effort.

A great plan and altruistic intentions mean nothing until you put energy and life behind them. If you are in business, you know that a business plan is simply a collection of ideas until you start executing — allocating resources, making decisions, hiring people, and solving problems. That's when you can see the plan come to life. That's when you can truly see how good your plan was and the impact it has.

Let's pause on the word "impact" for a moment. According to the dictionary, impact is "the force of impression of one thing on another : a significant or major effect."[6]

So if you want to know if someone is living their purpose, you look at the *results* of their decisions and actions, not just at their plans and their words. You look at the effects of their life on those around them.

We all know people who are big talkers. They claim they're going to get serious about getting in shape and start training for a marathon. They even proudly show you the running app on their phone with the plan they're going to follow. The next time you see them and ask how their training is going, they haven't actually done anything. "I'm choosing what race to sign up for," they say, or "It's been too hot to run, so I'm going to start when the weather cools down." But the next time you see them, you know it will be more of the same. The weather is bad, work has been busy, or it gets dark too early ... They're sure to have a list of very plausible excuses, all of which have prevented them from moving forward.

Here's the blunt truth: If others cannot see the actions and impact of your mission in your life, you are not yet living it.

Living your purpose is the point where your internal commitment becomes external, and that can be intimidating. What was once private, possibly shared with just a few trusted people, now becomes public. That invites comments, criticism, and advice — some wanted and useful, some not.

People watch the way you live. Your choices, particularly as a leader, are visible to others. They see what you put out into the world through your words and your behavior. That's what living your purpose is. And that, of course, includes the decisions that you make, how you treat people, what your priorities are, who you choose to spend time with, and where you put your money.

What judgments would people make about you by looking at your life? Where do you spend your time, your treasure, and your talents?

In this section, we'll talk about what it means to live your life purpose. Now that you have owned your mission, how does that drive your decision-making? What will you do when your mission comes in conflict with other priorities in your life? How do you handle setbacks and challenges? And who will you invite to support you on your journey?

The Bible talks a lot about the "fruit" of our lives. In other words, you can tell what kind of tree you are growing by the fruit it bears.

> *You will know them by their fruits. Do men gather grapes from thornbushes or figs from thistles? Even so, every good tree bears good fruit, but a bad tree bears bad fruit. A good tree cannot bear bad fruit, nor can a bad tree bear good fruit. Every tree that does not bear good fruit is cut down and thrown into the fire. Therefore by their fruits you will know them.*
> –Matt. 7:16-20, NKJV

Chapter 8

Living in Uncertainty

L iving your purpose means you need to shift from talking the talk to walking the walk. You need to be willing to change your life in order to live courageously and embody your mission. You must take those risks and turn them into reality, dealing with the impact they'll have on others and yourself. But with the risks come rewards, excitement, and the peace of knowing you are living the life you were designed to live.

The Moment of Launch

Think about a rocket launch. Thousands of different people are involved in the planning — designing the rocket, calculating the fuel needed for the journey, packing the meal rations into their proper places, training the astronauts, and even adhering the American flag to the shoulder of each and every space suit. But all of these steps and details only gain meaning when the countdown is complete, and the rocket takes off from Earth. That is the moment every piece of the plan comes together, and the whole world can see how good the plan actually was.

Your mission might not be as public as a rocket launch, but you're facing the same steps, from research to planning to execution.

Consider the leaders you've met in this book so far and when they started living their mission publicly. Michelle's moment came when she gathered a small group of people together to raise money for moms in tough situations. Gina's launch came when she decided to apply to a counseling program. Nathan's launch was deciding to follow his interest in alternative treatments for cancer and leave traditional medicine. Everyone has their own "launch" moment when they put their plans to the test.

What will your moment of launch look like? Through experience, I know that even if it seems like a small moment to others, to you, it will feel like you're taking a huge leap because you know what this step represents. You know that by making your commitment public, you're putting yourself on the line in a bigger way. You may wonder if you'll find your footing or if you've made a huge mistake and will fall flat on your face. That uncertainty is a natural part of taking a risk.

When doubt arises, trust in your preparation and planning. All the research, dreaming, and questioning have led you to this point. Now it's time to jump. If you're concerned things aren't going to go according to plan, let's set that worry aside because the answer is always "YES!"

Thriving as a leader in times of uncertainty requires a combination of two distinct skill sets I explain below. Your ability to develop these capabilities will determine whether you thrive or struggle when your carefully crafted plans fall apart or when something unseen arises on the horizon.

Anticipating the Unexpected

I'm a great planner. It's part of my mental DNA to analyze situations and lay out an efficient, effective path forward. I love schedules, to-do lists, and spreadsheets, but what's really allowed me to flourish in leadership positions is my ability to anticipate the unexpected.

That may sound counterintuitive. After all, the unexpected is ... well, unexpected!

Maybe a better way to phrase it is to simply say that I'm *anticipatory*. I don't just plan for when things go the most advantageous way; I create contingencies for other scenarios as well. I don't just ask, "What do I think will happen?" I also ask, "What might happen, and how will I handle it?"

At one point in my career, I needed to deal with a vice president who, on paper, was doing great. By any objective metric, he was killing it. But he was also killing his people on the way to "success." He had created such a hostile work environment that we were constantly receiving complaints about his behavior. I want to clarify that he wasn't acting in an illegal manner, which would have actually been easier in some ways because it would have been a black-and-white issue. Instead, he was just making people miserable. This mess was mine to deal with.

The challenge was that some people, particularly those above him in the org chart who only saw his results, really appreciated his approach and thought he was doing great. If I didn't remove him, though, I was allowing someone to erode our company culture. I decided that it didn't matter how great he looked on paper. The reality was that he was destroying the team, and he had to go.

I knew what the proper course of action was and why, but that wasn't enough. I also needed to anticipate what the pushback and questions would be from other invested parties. What would his supporters say? What questions would they ask? How could I demonstrate that I had made the right decision? What documentation would I need for backup? I thought all this through after I'd made my plan to ensure I had covered as many bases as possible. By the time I acted, I was fully prepared to answer any questions to back up my decision. It still wasn't easy. Some people still weren't happy, but they couldn't argue with what I'd done and why.

Even when writing this book, I'm anticipating who may pick it up and what questions readers might have. I want to do my best to think ahead to your situation and provide answers that will be useful. The more I'm able to do that; the more useful this book will be.

What questions can you anticipate? What problems might you run into? How can you respond effectively? Anticipating both the good and the bad as well as the expected and the unexpected is an inherent part of courageous leadership. When you demonstrate you have thought through your decisions, it's so much easier to show others that you know what you're doing and that your decisions are sound.

So, you may be thinking that anticipatory planning is all well and good when you know what the questions may be, but what do you do when something comes out of nowhere and blindsides you? What do you do when, say, a global pandemic forces you to close the doors on the business you just opened? Well, that's when you need to rely on the second essential skill: flexibility.

Bend, Don't Break

You already know that things don't go according to plan. And you probably already know that you can anticipate fifteen separate potential scenarios, playing out all the details for each … yet something completely different can always happen.

So what do you do when, despite your best efforts, you are confronted with circumstances you haven't even considered?

As a leader, know that a time will come when you're faced with a scenario you've never seen before and maybe one that you've never even thought about. That's when you need to rely on your flexibility and adjust to the situation on the fly.

Throughout my career, I became very accustomed to last-minute changes. The insurance industry is highly regulated, and it wasn't unusual for new company policies and requirements to be instituted seemingly out of the blue. Because many of the regulations occur at the state level, agents in different states could be facing very different requirements at the same time. This made for a challenging environment because things could change suddenly. As a result, I had to do my best to anticipate any upcoming changes. At the same time, I had to be flexible in order to keep my equilibrium when the unforeseen occurred. The last thing people want to see is confusion in their leader. They want to trust you and believe in you, especially in times of chaos.

Some people are naturally more flexible than others, but flexibility is a skill that can be learned and strengthened.

What I've found is that the more confident I am, the more flexible I can be. That confidence comes from three main sources.

Develop Your Strengths

First, as we talked about earlier in the book, it's important to know and invest in your skills and talents. When I know my strengths, it's easier to trust that I can respond effectively, even when faced with uncertainty.

For instance, after years of practice, I'm a very good public speaker. If I'm in the middle of a presentation and the sound goes out, my slideshow doesn't load properly, or someone in the audience starts being disruptive, I can handle it. It's not ideal, but because I've developed skills in this area, I know I can keep my cool, be flexible, and adjust.

Be Prepared

The next key to flexibility is preparation. Do your research and prepare for different scenarios. When I've done this, I have a better sense of how to react even when I'm faced with something unexpected. I've already thought through and considered various courses of events. While what is actually happening might not be exactly what I'd planned for, it will be close enough to provide some structure.

To continue with the presentation analogy, early in my career, a partner and I were giving a project briefing to a team of senior execs. For some reason, one person, in particular, decided it was his day to "get" me. He peppered me with challenging question after question, most with a negative undertone. My partner was left unscathed while I was under fire the entire time.

Because I'd thoroughly prepared, though, I was able to keep my calm in the midst of the onslaught. Was it fun? No way. I hadn't expected this attack, but I was able to deal with it professionally because of my prep work. I remained cool, answered appropriately and thoroughly, and won the respect of some of the others in the room, who actually approached me in private later to comment on what had occurred.

Focus on the Goal

The final key to flexibility is keeping your eye on the end goal. When I know what my desired outcome is, I can make effective decisions even when the specific plan has to be changed. My friend Ericka's situation is a great example of this principle. A single mom and talented manicurist, she had no idea that right after she decided to start her own salon in spring 2020 that the world would come to a standstill with a global pandemic.

Her mission was to create a business on her terms that would support her and her family, and serve her clients at the same time. She began to evaluate how she could reach that same outcome given the new restrictions under which she (and the rest of the country) were operating. Her solution: Rather than seeing the shutdown as a sign that she was on the wrong path, she used the time to prepare and make sure her plan was solid. She kept in communication with her clients via social media and digital marketing, and opened as soon as businesses got the thumbs-up. She never wavered from her goal of creating a successful business.

The best advice I can provide is to continue to use your values and priorities as a touchstone to return to in times of uncertainty and confusion. When you make decisions based on your values and the fruit you want to bear, you'll never go wrong.

I love this reminder of what a bold leader is called to do:

Who is wise and understanding among you? Let them show it by their good life, by deeds done in the humility that comes from wisdom.

–James 3:13 NIV

Chapter 9

Obstacles, Mistakes, and Failures

No matter how proficient we are as leaders or project managers, there's still a part of us that secretly wishes that things would go according to plan — at least once in a while!

Unfortunately, perfection doesn't exist, and our plans will go off-script more often than not. But what do we do when anticipation and flexibility aren't enough to get us through? What do we do when we're courageously reaching for that next stepping stone and what we thought was solid rock turns into mud?

That's what we'll tackle in this chapter: How to recover and continue in pursuit of our goals when we slip, slide, or do a complete face-plant. The good news is that while fumbles and frustrations are part of the process, they don't have to keep you from progressing. Let's talk about what failure is (and isn't) and how to lead through frustrations and setbacks.

The Purpose of Failure

Many people reject failure. They see it as something only other people are allowed to do.

Intuitively, we know this isn't true. We know everyone from Oprah Winfrey to Dave Ramsey has faced bankruptcies, firings, and product flops. Somehow, though, it can become almost unbearable when it's us who have to face our teams, our families, and possibly even the public at large.

So know this: The bigger and bolder the goal, the more likely you are to experience failure. You will face challenges, missteps, and outright face-plants in the pursuit of any goal. As a leader, one of the most important things you can do is to create a way to deal effectively with failure.

Now, I don't like failure any more than the next high achiever. However, I don't want the pain of mistakes and tumbles to be wasted. If I have to go through it, I'm going to get something from it. And here are three things I've determined:

1. **Failure is good for YOU.** Falling down can hurt. But if we never fell down, how would we ever learn or improve? If we are courageous enough to take risks and

then courageous enough to examine why things didn't work out as planned, we can learn, evolve, and grow into the person God meant us to be.

I don't know about you, but I'd hate to follow a leader who had never experienced a setback, challenge, or defeat. The leaders who have been tested are the ones with the greatest strengths and the ones others can trust to remain steady when the seas are rough.

2. **Failure is good for YOUR MISSION.** Failures, particularly early failures, can help avoid bigger problems later that could jeopardize the entire mission. Fighter pilots, for instance, can spend almost ten times as many hours in a simulator as they do in the cockpit of a real jet.[7] Why? Because they want to discover their errors in judgment and action before they're faced with a life-or-death situation (and it costs a lot less than repairing a fighter jet).

Failures can point out flaws in your plans and allow you to course correct, leading to a better outcome. If nothing ever went wrong and your plans weren't tested, the end result might not be the best it could be. By testing it and being willing to adjust, you can create a more effective result.

3. **Failure is good for OTHERS.** When you are a leader, it can be tempting to hide your flaws from others. When

you create a persona of shiny perfection, though, you sacrifice an opportunity to allow others to learn from your trials. You are also telling them that failure is not acceptable and that they should hide their own missteps. Not only does this contribute to a culture of fear, but it also prevents your team from sharing information and experiences that could benefit all.

Instead, if you are honest and authentic about the struggles you've gone through, you are inspiring others and teaching them how to behave in challenging times.

In sum, the old adage is true. You can learn more from your failures than from your successes … if you choose to. As the Bible says,

> Say to them, 'This is what the Lord says: "When people fall down, do they not get up? When someone turns away, do they not return?"'
>
> —Jer. 8:4, NIV

Embracing Humility

In the spirit of transparency, I want to share one of my biggest failures and how a spirit of humility helped me turn a tough situation into a win.

I was transferred to an underperforming region in the country, which just so happened to be on the West Coast. My nature as a leader is to roll up my sleeves and jump right in, but my personality and what had worked for me in previous situations didn't work as I had planned. For a full year, my numbers were in the basement, near or at the bottom of the nation, even though I'd been near the top in previous roles. Compounding the situation was the fact that when I accepted the new role, I was told by my supervisor that two key executives in the region were "untouchable." In other words, my job was to change the results but not to change much else.

I started wondering if there was an insurmountable mismatch between my style and the company as a whole, and several people close to me actually advised me to leave. I was committed to doing the job I was hired for, though. I began by taking a look in the mirror and getting honest and humble about the fact that something needed to change and that something was me. I had to adapt my leadership style to the environment if I wanted to see results.

What happened next was a brutal exercise called "Stop, Start, Continue." At its most basic, it involves another executive leading a meeting with my team without me present and asking them what they wanted me to stop doing as a leader, what they wanted me to start doing, and what I was doing right that they thought I should continue. Usually, these take an hour or two. Mine went on for five hours. Five hours where they tore apart everything from my style of dress (too formal for the West Coast, I was told) and my energy level (too enthusiastic).

When the facilitator gave me the feedback, I could have resisted or just given up. Instead of fighting back or defending myself, though, I adopted a position of humility and accepted their input as valid. If I wanted results with this team, I would have to change because they weren't going to change first. Because I was committed to the outcome, I committed to becoming a different type of leader, and it worked. It was the hardest time of my career, but it also became one of my greatest accomplishments and greatest learning experiences in my life — all because I was willing to embrace humility.

Looking back, I see the positive fruit of my willingness to learn and grow. At the end of the day, they knew I was willing to fight for them; I just needed to adjust my approach. Many tears were shed when I left the region, and I'm still in touch with many of these team members today.

All Failures Aren't Equal

Think about the following three scenarios someone might encounter in the pursuit of their dream:

- You're about to go live for your first-ever training session, and your internet goes out unexpectedly.

- You hire an acquaintance's PR team to handle public relations for the book you just wrote. After six months, you're met with a large invoice but zero results.
- Three years after trying to launch your new healthy snack bar to market, you are out of money and have to close your business.

All three of these situations might be considered failures, but if we dig deeper, we'll see that they're actually distinct from one another.

As you pursue your goal, you will encounter three types of setbacks. I sort them into obstacles, mistakes, and failures.

1. Obstacles

Let's start with obstacles. By definition, an obstacle is "something that impedes progress or achievement."[8] Obstacles occur when we are on the right path, but something is getting in our way. They are simply part of life because there will be elements of our plan we cannot control, no matter how much we try. From faulty technology to getting a "no" from a prospective client, obstacles are incidents that temporarily block our way to our goal. The question to ask yourself when you hit an obstacle is, "What can I do to overcome the obstacle?" Usually, there are other ways around the obstacle to your end goal. For instance, there are other clients to work with, other banks to ask for financing, and other ways to get your message into the world.

When you hit an obstacle, regroup and use your creativity and determination to devise a new route to your dream.

2. Mistakes

Next, let's consider mistakes. The dictionary defines a mistake as "a wrong action or statement proceeding from faulty judgment, inadequate knowledge, or inattention."[9] When you make a mistake, you miss something you probably should have seen or anticipated. You used the wrong formula to calculate pricing, you showed up at the Marriott when your meeting was at the Marquis, or you made another error that ended up costing you time, money, or another resource.

When you screw up, the question you should ask yourself is, "How can I recover from this?" Sometimes it's backing up and moving forward, like if you take the wrong exit on a highway and end up at a dead end. Other times, it requires saying you're sorry, cleaning up your mess, and moving on. Still other times, you may not be able to — or may not need to — fully recover, so you just move forward the best you can.

Everyone makes mistakes. Own what happened, resolve not to make the same mistake moving forward, and let it go.

3. Failures

Failures are the most feared of the three setbacks. A failure is a "lack of success: a failing in business : bankruptcy : a falling short : deficiency."[10] No one wants to be seen as deficient! But when I work with my clients, I urge them not to view a failure as a reflection of their character. It is part of the journey rather than the end of the journey. It's what happens *after* the failure that says more about you than the failure itself.

If you have put your heart and soul (and money and time) into the pursuit of your vision and feel like things are simply not working out, you have some questions to ask yourself. Is the "no" really a "not yet"? Maybe your plan is a solid one, but you simply need more time or money for it to come to fruition. Or maybe you need a different strategy, as I did when I was head of the West Coast region; no matter how hard I tried, the approach I was using just wasn't going to work. In some cases, you may have tried your best, but you aren't going to reach your goal. That's the most difficult situation to accept, but please realize that there is achievement in trying. What you have learned will serve you in your future endeavors.

When you run into "problems" or issues, don't automatically assume a slip is an insurmountable crash. Give yourself time to catch your breath, and then evaluate. Is this an obstacle to which you need to strategize a new approach? Is it an error in judgment that led to a mistake? Or is it truly a failure? All three happen to all of us.

Whatever the situation, don't rush to cover it up. Instead, extract whatever meaning you can from it. Brave leaders learn from their challenges. Use the difficult periods to build your strength and stamina because, in the pursuit of a worthy goal, there are always more challenges ahead.

Chapter 10

Creating Your Support Team

Leadership can feel lonely, particularly if you are on a bold mission in uncharted territory. But you don't have to be isolated in pursuit of your dreams. Yes, you might be the figurehead and the one forging the way, but that doesn't mean you have to do it all on your own. In this chapter, we'll take a look at the people who can support you as you move forward and organize them into four distinct groups.

As we go through these different roles, you may discover that you have all of these people in your life right now, and you just weren't aware of the role they were playing — or had a term for it. You also might discover that you have a bunch of blanks when it comes to naming who you have in your corner. Remember that this is the "ideal" list, not necessarily the practical one. There were times in my career when I operated without a full slate of support people. If you're in a similar situation, it will be much easier to fill those gaps now that you have identified what you're looking for.

A Steady Hand

The first category I want to address is that of a mentor. By definition, a mentor is "a trusted counselor or guide."[11] A mentor is somebody who is there for advice. You can reach out as needed and share a sticky work situation. They'll help you process the situation and work with you to decide how you can best respond. As experienced guides, mentors can also help you avoid landmines while working toward your goals. Their unofficial role is to help you develop as a leader and as a person.

The biggest question people have about mentoring is how to find one.

Some organizations have structured mentor programs where you're matched with a mentor. This arrangement has pluses and minuses. On the upside, you have a ready-made mentor. The minus: You may or may not connect with the mentor you've been assigned.

For that reason, I advocate locating your own mentor so you can choose someone you feel connected with and whom you trust. Trust is essential because you're going to be vulnerable with them, so you want to be assured that they will keep your conversations confidential and that they'll also have your best interest at heart.

One of my most impactful mentors in the corporate world was my coworker Shirley. She worked in a different division, and I was always impressed with her analytical brain and great personality. I wanted to relate better to my operations peers, so I asked her to mentor me. Specifically, I wanted her to provide feedback on how I came across in meetings and how I could be more effective. She agreed, and we regularly talked after joint meetings to analyze my performance. Her input wasn't always fun to hear, but she helped me develop in areas I knew I needed to grow as a leader.

When you find someone you'd like to mentor you, simply ask them directly: "I think you are amazing at what you do, and my goal is to become more effective at _____. Would you be willing to mentor me?" Then, as I did with Shirley, let them know specifically what you would like them to do and what the relationship would look like. Sometimes, people aren't sure or don't feel they'll be able to give you the time required. Don't take it personally; find someone else and keep trying. The relationship is worth it. Over two decades later, Shirley and I are still friends, and she still calls me "Mentee!"

Fighting for You

Another relationship that's invaluable is that of a champion. The dictionary defines a champion as "a militant advocate or defender; one that does battle for another's rights or honor."[12]

While you may not ask your champion to go into battle for you, you will want them on your side.

A champion in the business world is someone who believes in your skills and potential. They will consistently put your name forth when opportunities for advancement arise. Having an advocate who is higher up on the org chart or in an effective position to recommend you as you pursue your goals is invaluable. Many hiring and promotion decisions are made years in advance, even before they're made public. If you don't have someone fighting for you, you can be seriously disadvantaged.

It's rare to approach someone directly and say, "Hey, wanna be my champion?" Instead, this relationship usually develops over time by consistently meeting and exceeding expectations. When I was an insurance agent in Ohio, the person in charge of our region was a senior vice president, Cal. I got on his radar because I quickly became one of the top agents in Ohio and then one of the top agents in the country. Cal noticed, and he promoted me through multiple levels, championing me for advancement after advancement.

We never talked about it. He never coached me. I never called him for advice. I just knew what he was looking for, and I did it. He believed in me. He put my name forward for promotions, and he took risks for me because he knew I'd deliver.

In turn, as I moved up the ranks in the company, I got a reputation as a developer of future leaders. I was skilled at identifying talent and working with people to prepare them for the next level. Once I saw what someone was capable of, I'd go all out for them. It was a win-win-win situation: a win for the company, a win for the future leader, and a win for me.

If you're not in a corporate environment, it's still critical to have a champion. In fact, I'm a champion for several people now. Every time I come across someone who needs their services or expertise or I hear of an opportunity that would benefit them or I am introduced to someone they need to meet, I put their name forth. I believe in them, and I know they won't let me down, just as Cal knew I wouldn't let him down.

It's important to remember that champions are risking their reputation for you. If they suggest or refer you and you don't perform, you make them look bad. That's why the best way to find a champion is to go above and beyond in everything you do, and often your champion will find you. If there is someone who is in a position to put your name forward in the area you want to move, ask for feedback. If it's positive, say, "Thank you so much. My goal is to _____. I would appreciate it if you could mention me as a potential candidate if any opportunities come up." If you're performing above your level, they'll notice.

In the Trenches

One of the support categories you might be most familiar with is a coach or "a private tutor; one who instructs or trains."[13]

The idea of hiring a coach to help with personal or professional goals has become much more commonplace in the last decade.

Coaches are distinct from mentors and champions in several key ways. First, most coach relationships are clearly transactional. You hire a coach and pay them to help you achieve a specific goal or to coach you for a specific period of time. Second, the coach should have experience achieving the goal you aspire to. For instance, if you hire a coach to help you start a nonprofit, write a book, or take your business to seven figures, they should have gotten those results with other clients in the past.

I work with a variety of clients on very specific goals, including presentation and public speaking skills, leadership, and image — all areas where I have a track record of success. Some clients work with me for several months, while others may be with me for a year or more. It all depends on their goals and their timeline.

You can do an internet search for a coach to work with, but the best way to find a coach is through referral. Many of my clients find their way to me because a mutual friend or colleague recommended me. Ask people you respect if they have any names they can suggest. Because the coaching industry is unregulated, make sure to do your due diligence. Ask the coach about their experiences, who they've worked with in the past, and what kind of results they've had with people with similar goals. While one-on-one coaching is not inexpensive, it's one of the best investments you can make in your mission and in yourself. If Serena Williams hires a tennis coach and Faith Hill has a vocal coach, shouldn't high-level leaders have coaches, too?

On-Call Support

What does almost every high-wire performer have to ensure they land safely, even when they make a misstep? Their net, of course.

A net, by definition, is "an open-meshed fabric twisted, knotted, or woven together at regular intervals."[14] Some people might also call it your network, but I'm using the term very specifically. When I talk about your "net," I don't mean everyone you've ever exchanged business cards with, but those who offer specific types of expertise and whom you can call on when you have particular challenges or questions.

Think of your net as a group of advisors and experts who can assist you as needed. Your net may overlap with the other three categories, but not necessarily. In a given year, you may never need some members of your net, while you may connect with other members five times or more. It all depends on what assistance you need in pursuit of your mission.

When I was in the corporate world, my net included a woman who was my counterpart in Canada as well as the head of all attorneys for the company. My mentor Shirley was in my net, but my champion Cal was not. Now that I've left the corporate world, my net has changed accordingly. I have people to assist me with book writing and publishing questions, people to reach out to regarding women in leadership, people to connect with regarding politics, and many other issues.

Creating your net is simple. If you meet someone you enjoy and feel you can provide value to, and vice-versa, just ask: "I enjoyed meeting you. Would it be okay if I reached out to you in the future if I have any questions about _____?" Remember, powerful leaders don't have to know everything, but they know where to go when they need answers. That's what your net is for.

Caring for Your People

One thing I want to stress as we round up this discussion of your support team is the idea that while people are resources, they are, first and foremost, *individuals.* Like all humans, they want to be appreciated. How you care for them and these valuable relationships will determine how long they will continue to be part of your support network.

The relationship with your coach is straightforward because it is based on a clear exchange of value: You hire them and pay them a predetermined amount for a predetermined period of time. Often, there's even a contract or agreement that you'll both sign to lay out these expectations.

But with the rest of your support team, you might be wondering what's in it for them. For instance, why did Shirley agree to be my mentor? Why did Cal champion me? Why do people take my calls when I have questions about accounting, publishing, or health?

There is a lack of leaders with ambition and drive in our world, and people want to be part of something positive. When others hear that you're interested in creating something bold in the world, they want to work alongside you. When I shared my career goals with Shirley, she was inspired. Your dreams will likewise inspire those around you who want to use their experience to support you.

As my champion, Cal knew that if I succeeded, I'd make him look good as well. Just as I became known in later years as a developer of leaders, he could grow a reputation for championing excellent people, too.

And as for your net, people need each other, especially when working toward large goals.. By helping you with a question on setting up a website, for example, a colleague knows they can reach out for help in your area of expertise. It's this kind of quid pro quo that makes the world go around.

Finally, treat your support team and everyone you encounter with respect and appreciation. These individuals are spending their most valuable resource with you — their time. Even if they can't support you in the way you might wish, they still deserve gratitude. You'll never be sorry for being polite and respectful and saying, "Thank you."

I'll end this chapter with a verse on the value of your team: *"Plans fail for lack of counsel, but with many advisers they succeed"* (Prov. 15:22, NIV). With your support people in place, you're on the path to success.

PART THREE WRAP-UP

As you LIVE into your calling, you'll face challenges, setbacks, and more likely than not, failures as well. That is part of being a leader and forging paths that few have been courageous enough to tread.

What I want you to take from this section is that though you may feel uncertain, anxious, or even scared, you don't have to move forward unprepared or on your own. By starting with your reasons for venturing forth, reviewing your life values, and anticipating challenges, you'll be ready to make the decisions you need to in order to bring your mission to reality.

Along the way, your boldness will inspire others. They'll see you act with conviction and confidence, even in the face of challenges and threats, and you will light a fire within them. Some may become part of your support system while others will observe from afar — but people are watching.

We live in an age of demotivation, depression, separation, and even despair. It's rare to see someone boldly proclaim their beliefs, particularly when they may go against the common narrative. You can be certain that as you pursue your goals, you are illuminating the path for others. That's what we'll discuss in more detail in the next section as we talk about how to DUPLICATE your efforts for greater impact.

The light shines in the darkness, and the darkness has not overcome it.

–1 John 3:5, NIV

DUPLICATE IT

We've come a long way on our journey together, and we've covered a lot of ground.

So far, we've talked about the need to **Believe** that you are meant to step out and create something more in your life. We've discussed what it means to **Own** that calling in your life. We then talked about what is involved when you **Live** that purpose. Now, in our final section, we'll explore how you can **Duplicate** your mission by both bringing others along with you and by inspiring them to do more with their own lives. As part of this discussion, we'll talk about what it means to embrace and pass on the torch of leadership.

But before we can do that, I want to bring up an important question: *What is a leader?*

That may seem like a strange thing to ask, especially since we're already deep into a discussion on bold leadership ... but I really want you to think about the answer to this question.

Most people will automatically respond that a leader is someone who has followers. While that might be technically accurate, leadership goes beyond a title or a box on an organizational chart. True leadership is a condition of the heart, not just what your business card says.

While I believe that everyone can be a leader in some capacity in their lives, I also believe that only a few have been chosen to be bold leaders — and fewer still will accept that commission for their lives. As we've seen in previous chapters, plenty of people feel pulled by a hint of a dream, yet they still decline the opportunity to step forward and lead courageously. They see the risk and discomfort as too high a price to pay and choose to stay where they are instead of venturing into the unknown.

But not you ... which is why we're here together.

You have a yearning inside you that seems to defy logic. It's a pull that comes back to you — again and again. It's a pull that you cannot ignore, despite knowing the sacrifices you may be called to make. And that is what makes you bold.

Having the "authority" to lead isn't enough. When you lead from your heart and mind, you want others to follow you from their hearts and minds as well. That means your impact on them goes beyond that granted by a title or job requirement. You offer true influence, and that comes only when others willingly allow you to guide them.

When you reach that level of trust and openness, you not only impact the world through your mission, but you also inspire others to step forward and believe, own, and live their own life purpose.

Let me explain it in another way. I love to bake (I'm Italian; it's in my genes!), so I'll use baking as an example.

Let's say I decide to make cinnamon rolls one Saturday morning. I assemble all the ingredients on my kitchen counter and get to work. At first, maybe my husband, Ed, hears the rattling of dishes and the mixer, but nothing really interrupts his day or grabs his attention ... yet. A bit later, though, when I actually put the cinnamon rolls in the oven, the smell of sugary goodness permeates our condo, and he knows something big is happening. By the time I pull the rolls out of the oven, he's ready with a knife and fork, and his mouth is watering!

The impact of my cooking project doesn't stop there, though. If the cinnamon smell sneaks into the hall and under the front door to our neighbors' condo, or they catch a whiff of heaven when they get off the elevator, they might be hoping I'll deliver some warm rolls when they're ready (I'm known for sharing the wealth!). Even more, the next time *they* make some goodies, they might remember how much they appreciated the treat and be moved to share with their friends as well. My Saturday baking has turned into a cascade of good deeds.

As a mission-driven leader, you're like a baker in the kitchen. Others pick up on what you're doing, and even if you're not directly "leading" them, you impact them by your example and improve their day by sharing your projects, goals, and accomplishments. Most importantly, through your efforts, you're inspiring, demonstrating what it means to embrace their own calling. Your actions truly speak louder than words!

In the following chapters, we're going to lay the groundwork to make it easier for others to "catch" your inspiration. We'll look at how to encapsulate your purpose in an easy-to-understand way. We'll talk about sharing your mission more broadly (and how to deal with critics who are bound to pop up). And in our final chapter together, we'll look at some essential characteristics of bold leadership so you can have a reminder to take with you into your future endeavors.

Chapter 11

Defining Your Mission

In the past chapters, we spent a lot of time talking about your purpose as it relates to you and God. While you may have enlisted the support of a few key people, you haven't necessarily gone public with your mission. It's been pretty invisible ... until now!

Now is the time to start sharing your dreams with a wider audience, even if it's a bit intimidating. After all, to create a movement and be a leader, you need others to join in your efforts. We're going to break the process down to make it as simple as possible to share your vision and get others on board.

The first step involves being able to explain to others what you're doing and where you're going. If you cannot paint a vivid, compelling picture of what you want to accomplish, you're going to have a very hard time convincing others to support you. Whether you're looking for financing from a bank, soliciting donations from individuals, or speaking to a team of potential volunteers, you need to have your mission dialed in. How you talk about your work is a key contributor to your success.

Painting the Picture: The Importance of Vision

Have you ever seen a commercial and thought to yourself, "What was that all about?" While the visuals might have been eye-catching, you couldn't figure out what was being advertised. Shaving cream? A new meal delivery service? A cruise to Alaska? By the time the next commercial comes on, you've forgotten what the first one was about because it didn't make any sense.

It's not uncommon for advertisers and brands to confuse creativity with effectiveness. Just because people watch your ad doesn't mean they're going to buy your product — especially if they can't figure out what you're selling. The same goes for our personal missions. If people don't know what we're trying to accomplish, they're going to have a hard time caring about what we're doing. That's why, as leaders, we must be skilled at sharing our visions.

As King Solomon, believed to be the author of the book of Proverbs, wrote: "Where there is no vision, the people perish" (Prov. 29:18, KJV). While he was talking about God's vision for mankind, the principle holds true on an individual level. While people might not literally die if you can't share your vision in a powerful way, your dream might die because no one will pay attention. There are simply too many distractions in our modern world to expect people to listen to you if you're not communicating effectively.

Look at the stats: In the 1970s, Americans were exposed to an estimated 500 to 1,600 ads per day. Today, we see an astounding 4,000 to 10,000 ads each and every 24-hour period.[15] Keep in mind: These stats don't include texts, social media posts, 24/7 news channels, work emails, and the thousands of other attention-stealers competing with you to grab people's minds and hearts.

The key to breaking through this noise is being able to communicate your vision to others in a concise, meaningful way. I'm not talking about a slogan like Nike's "Just Do It" or Apple's "Think Different." Nor am I talking about bloated corporate mission statements that are often created by committees and then forgotten until it's time to write the annual report. Instead, I'm talking about the equivalent of an elevator pitch — a short, simple declaration of your purpose that others can easily understand. Let's call it your purpose statement to distinguish it from a corporate mission statement.

Think back to Michelle Moore, whom you met in chapter 7. Michelle felt the calling to help other women. If you ran into her and asked her about her organization, Mother's Grace, she'd be able to tell you in a sentence: "Mother's Grace is a charity that supports mothers and families who are in acute crisis." Of course, there's a lot more to share, but that simple sentence gets to the heart of her mission.

Let me share another example from my friend Carol Robbins, the owner of Pearl Med Spa located in Portland and Scottsdale. Carol is crystal-clear on the purpose behind her business: "We're a ministry disguised as a med spa." Every staff member knows their goal is to serve and minister to the women and men who come through their doors, showing them the love of Christ.

Both these women have mastered the art of sharing their vision in a short, straightforward manner. Their descriptions are easy to understand yet invite the listener to ask for more — exactly the right way to engage others.

Being able to do the same for your mission is a combination of being clear on your values, sharing your passion, and communicating your goals. While these three elements might not be specifically mentioned in your purpose statement, they are the foundation. Once you understand those three building blocks, you can create a simple statement like Michelle's or Carol's.

Back to Basics

Sharing your purpose with others starts with your "why." Why, out of all the ways you could spend your time and out of all the calls for your attention, did you choose this particular endeavor? The answer to this question lies in your values. Without having to ask them, I know that Michelle values community and service, and Carol is driven by her Christian faith. What about you? What are your values, and how are you demonstrating them through your mission?

Your purpose statement should be a bridge between your values and your vision. When people hear your purpose statement, they should intuitively understand what is important to you and what your goals are.

In chapter 2, I shared some stories that gave a glimpse into my values, including honoring God, personal responsibility, and encouraging others. Those values underlie my purpose statement as a coach, which is to help others step into their greatness. When people who know me well but haven't seen me for a while hear what I'm now working on professionally, they're never surprised. Instead, I hear, "That is perfect for you!" or, "Wow, that makes so much sense." That's because my values — which have remained constant over the course of my career — naturally led me to my next step of coaching.

If you haven't taken the time to do the exercises in chapter 2, please do so now. These short exercises are essential tools for moving forward with your mission. Then, think about how your bold calling as a leader is an expression of those values. Remember: Every decision you make as a leader stems from your values. It's a good idea to get clear on what's influencing you!

The Power of Passion

A mistake many leaders make, particularly those with a corporate background, is sapping all the emotion from their communication. They are concerned with being taken seriously and appearing "professional." As a result, they tone down their feelings. This is a mistake because emotions are largely what move people to action. If you can appeal to people's emotions, you can pull them into your mission.

When I think about "passion," my client, Dr. Nathan Goodyear, the vitamin C expert, always comes to mind. All it takes is a short conversation with him to hear his fervor for health and healing, and to sense the responsibility he feels as a doctor. He'll tell you about new discoveries in the application of vitamin C to cancer treatment, and he'll probably also talk about how the word "doctor" in Hebrew means "healer." Nathan, quite simply, wants to heal people, and he'll gladly tell you about his patients and their successes.

Nathan knows that stories are an excellent way to tap into emotions and to get people's attention. It's hard to make people feel strong emotions simply by sharing facts and data, but when you share stories — yours or others' — you activate the hippocampus, the part of the brain responsible for learning and memory.[16] Carol Robbins and Michelle Moore know this intuitively. They can share dozens of stories about the women they've supported through their organizations and then connect these to their own personal stories of why they do what they do.

In this book, I've done the same by sharing many stories about my clients and friends in order to bring my words to life. I want you to remember the principles we've discussed, and the best way to do that is by illustrating them with vivid stories.

Stories move people to action. Think about what stories you can tell, both from your own history and from the people you've worked with and helped. Don't be hesitant to share emotions, too. After all, your mission is about emotion as well as logic. Passion is appealing!

Eyes on the Prize

Stories aren't just a great way to make your mission come alive for others. They're also an effective tool for showing others your end goal. People have a difficult time remembering concepts they don't understand. By telling others about what you've worked on and what you've accomplished, you fill in the gaps and make it easier for them to relate to your mission.

When Michelle talks about a single mom who was diagnosed with cancer and reached out to Mother's Grace for assistance, it's easy for a listener to understand what Mother's Grace is all about. When Nathan shares a story about a client with breast cancer whose tumors shrank in size after being treated with a course of intravenous vitamin C, we know immediately what his goal is. After Carol talks about the philanthropy Pearl Med Spa has undertaken (including building an orphanage in Tonga), you know this is no ordinary med spa but one making a difference in the larger world.

What stories do you have to demonstrate your goals? What success stories or case studies can you share? Even if you're in the early stages, you can still share stories. Talk about how your trip to India opened your eyes to the plight of orphaned girls in Mumbai or how your struggles to find quality after-school care made you determined to help other parents. People want to know what you're doing, but they also want to know why you're doing it.

Putting It Together

If you're feeling a little overwhelmed by the process of coming up with a short, snappy statement about your calling, that's absolutely natural. It can be difficult to encapsulate everything you want to say into just a sentence or two. Give yourself room to explore and experiment.

Remember, your goal isn't to summarize everything you do and why and how you do it; your goal is to provide just enough of a teaser so that people get the big picture. They should understand your larger goal and, hopefully, want to learn more.

Think about this in terms of your profession. You wouldn't attempt to tell someone all about your education, your full resume, and your career goals in a simple cocktail party exchange. Instead, you might tell them you're an attorney specializing in intellectual property or that you're a corporate real estate agent. You're giving a bit of information to allow them to understand the big picture, and then, they can ask for more.

That's the same thing I want to prepare you to do with your purpose statement: Offer a teaser to get people headed in the right direction, and then when they're intrigued, you can back it up with stories illustrating your passion and expertise.

Communicating something as important as your personal calling can be challenging. Don't expect to get it right immediately. Practice talking about your mission and see where it takes you. Note what kinds of questions people ask, where they seem to get confused, and where they seem to "get" it. One of the best responses you can receive is when their eyes light up, and they say, "I know someone who needs to talk with you!" When someone else shows emotion, you're doing something right.

Humans have an innate urge to classify. When we confuse others through contradictory statements, unclear language, or overwhelm, they don't know what "box" to put us in. Sometimes, they'll take the time to ask questions, but in today's world, it's more likely that they'll just move on. That's why the clearer you can be, the more effective you are.

Chapter 12

Going Public

I remember the first time I was asked to give a quarterly accountability presentation for the company's CEO and executive team. I had attended these virtual video calls many times over the previous two years, and I took mental notes of what went well and what didn't. What confused attendees? When was more information better than less? What's the best way to preempt or address topics that might be controversial?

When I was promoted to Senior VP, it was my turn to put all my research to the test. After hours of preparation and practice, I was as ready as possible. My predecessor had been a numbers guy, known as the smartest person in the organization. Big shoes to fill, but I trusted my gut and my preparation. I anticipated questions that the attendees might have and took care to present information in logical, digestible chunks. I told my team that our goal was to address any objections before they arose, leaving nothing to chance.

As I wrapped up my review, I thought it had gone well ... but a presentation is only as good as the audience thinks it is. Fortunately, the CEO agreed. "This is the best call we've ever had, and this is how all of them should be run," he said. My team's hard work had paid off.

That presentation occurred over ten years ago, and I would go on to give dozens of presentations online and in person to groups of all sizes. But please don't think for a moment that all of my speaking engagements have been smash hits.

In fact, I've been on stage in front of a thousand people when my presentation seemed to fall apart. I was scheduled to speak at a conference for a primary college for financial education, and as a favor, the president of the college asked me to copresent with a newer agent. I didn't know him personally, but the president assured me he was very sharp. My copresenter and I planned out our talk, and I trusted all was well. But it wasn't long into our presentation when things went off the rails. It was clear we were on two different wavelengths. The content appeared disjointed and clunky, and the audience didn't connect to our material.

Afterward, I received feedback from a valued member of my net (see chapter 10). She said, "Deb, that just did not work. You two were completely unmatched in terms of skill and knowledge. Don't do that again." Lesson learned — the hard way. And even though it had been painful, I survived. So will you.

Nothing to Fear

With stories like that, you may wonder why I — or anyone — willingly set foot onto a stage or take the podium in front of a group of any size. After all, public speaking is cited as a fear in almost 75 percent of the population, making it one of the most common phobias.[17] If you're speaking boldly about a potentially controversial or groundbreaking topic, the stress can be even greater.

Maybe you feel like Moses did when God told him that he was to be the leader of the Israelites:

> *Moses said to the Lord, "Pardon your servant, Lord. I have never been eloquent, neither in the past nor since you have spoken to your servant. I am slow of speech and tongue."*
>
> —Ex. 4:10, NIV

Moses knew what all leaders know: it's a risk to stand in front of a group. All eyes are on you, and you're opening yourself up to judgment. Being singled out can go against our natural impulse to blend in for security. We might be reluctant to be in the spotlight if it means we might be judged or criticized.

Even my client Lisa, the former crew chief in the Army, admits to getting a bit anxious before giving presentations — and she led troops and worked on military helicopters! In other words, even the most courageous of us can feel a bit anxious at the thought of speaking in front of groups, particularly about a topic that we're passionate about.

Still, speaking publicly about your mission is one of the most powerful actions you can take not only to spread the word about your efforts but also to grow as a leader. Also, with the right preparation and mindset, you can learn to enjoy (or at least not hate) speaking in public.

Why You Need to Take the Stage

Talking to groups, hosting a training, being interviewed on a podcast, doing a book reading, or appearing on traditional media channels like TV and radio are all tools you can use to recruit volunteers, enlist support, and spread the word about your mission. Additionally, when your movement starts to gain traction and people hear your story, they will naturally want to invite you to share with a larger audience.

My friend and client Martha kept quiet about her story of domestic violence for most of her life. Once she started talking about her experiences escaping an abusive relationship and rebuilding her life, though, people wanted to listen. She was invited to speak to larger audiences, appear on podcasts, and share her story more widely. Her message resonated with women and men going through their own struggles, and she was able to serve as an inspiration for them.

Martha learned that speaking publicly about your story can benefit you and your mission in several ways. First, the more people who are exposed to your message, the more people you can positively impact. You never know who in the audience is in a position to support you or who needs to hear you because of what they're going through in their own life.

Talking publicly about your passion also makes the subject come alive to the audience. There's a huge difference between reading a website or brochure about domestic violence and hearing Martha speak firsthand. Your audience can hear the emotion and authenticity in your voice, and as we discussed earlier, emotion moves people to act. Sharing yourself so publicly may make you feel vulnerable, but it's that vulnerability that will connect with the public.

Next, the more you speak about your calling, the better communicator you'll become. Communication is a process, one in which you'll become more skilled the more you do it. Even though my first briefing went well, my future ones were even better as I learned more about presenting and became more confident. Give yourself the ability to grow by speaking and presenting regularly.

Finally, speaking opportunities lead to other speaking opportunities. My physician client, Nathan, whom I've mentioned several times, has seen a chain effect when it comes to sharing his mission with others. After speaking at one conference, he was invited to speak at another and then another in short order. Now, he wants to make public speaking an essential part of his schedule in order to bring more visibility to using vitamin C in oncology. The more effective you are at speaking, the more likely you'll be to get additional invitations. After all, most people don't want the pressure of stepping onto a stage, so if you're willing and good at it, you can expect to receive more requests.

Making the Most of the Opportunity

It's impossible to sum up how to be a good speaker in just a few pages. There are hundreds of books on public speaking, and I often work one-on-one with my clients for several months to prepare them for large-scale, high-stakes presentations. However, there are some specific principles that can help you make the most of any speaking opportunity, no matter how large or small the audience. The principles are preparation, practice, and a positive mindset.

First, preparation. We've talked about preparation and being anticipatory in previous chapters, so it's no surprise that great speakers prepare for their talks. *How* expert speakers prepare may surprise you, though.

Here are areas to address when preparing:

Content. It's not enough to know your material. You also need to consider how you're going to structure and present your content. When Martha started getting more invitations to talk to larger audiences, she wanted to make sure she was sharing her story in an effective manner. We worked together to create a compelling narrative that was moving and logically structured. Our goal was to leave the audience inspired.

Format. A two-hour, in-person, moderated panel Q&A session is very different from a 15-minute solo presentation. To prepare effectively, you must know the length of your talk, the structure, if there will be time for questions, and so on. These are all details that a newer speaker might not think to clarify, but they can significantly affect your talk.

Venue and Technology. Likewise, you want to know all the details about where you'll be speaking. How large is the room? Is there a stage and/or podium? Will you have a microphone? Will it be handheld or hands-free? Will there be a screen for your slides? Do you need to bring your own computer? Will they have the necessary adapters to hook your laptop to the projector? Will people be seated at tables banquet-style, or in seats facing the front, as in a theater? These details may not seem important, but when you are counting on walking freely as you speak, only to find out you're stuck at the podium microphone, it can really throw you off. Knowing beforehand allows you to prepare accordingly.

Audience. There are some speakers who give the same talk, regardless of the occasion or audience. If you simply go on autopilot when handed a microphone, though, you're missing an opportunity to connect with the audience. Get as much information about them as possible. Is the occasion a pump-them-up motivational meeting or a gathering of top executives to address poor quarterly performance numbers? Are you speaking to experts or the general public? Is this a "friendly" audience or one that's more likely to have tough questions? What are their big concerns and interests? What is the audience's average age? The more you can understand their mindset, the better you'll be able to adjust your presentation to their wants and needs.

Beyond Preparation

Many people think they need to memorize their talk word-for-word. Most experts advise against this because it can come across as robotic, and it also keeps you from responding in the moment to the audience. On the flip side, you also don't want to read your speech. The best approach is to know your material so well that you can present it naturally but not so well that you sound recorded. It's a tough balance to strike ... which is why you need to practice!

Practicing means rehearsing *everything* about your talk, including using the clicker to forward your slides, where you're going to stand, how you're going to move, when you will pause, and how you will take questions. For some of my clients, I'll even adopt the role of a challenging audience member and ask tough questions so they'll be prepared with their answers. Simulate the event as much as possible.

Finally, let's talk about dealing with nerves. The best way you can allay any anxiety is by adopting a positive mindset, reinforcing that you've prepared and practiced for this moment. Remind yourself of your purpose: to convey valuable information to an audience who wants to be inspired and take action.

At the beginning of this chapter, I told you how Moses told God he wasn't a good speaker. Now let's hear God's answer:

> *The Lord said to him, "Who gave human beings their mouths? Who makes them deaf or mute? Who gives them sight or makes them blind? Is it not I, the Lord? Now go; I will help you speak and will teach you what to say."*
>
> –Exod. 4:11, NIV

When you have a purpose placed on your heart and a calling placed on your life, God is guiding you. Trust that the one who created you will help you speak.

Chapter 13

The Bold Leader's List

When you think of courageous leaders, who comes immediately to mind? Consider the most compelling leaders you know, the ones you'd trust with your life. Whether your list includes iconic figures from the past or people you have encountered throughout your life, great leaders share some similarities. These shared characteristics can serve as touchpoints for you as you develop as a leader.

In this chapter, we'll review the qualities I believe to be essential for bold leaders and why. One note: This is my list of the top 15 characteristics great leaders share. While many of the leadership traits I identify are universal, some may be more in line with my personal experiences. As you go through the list, note your own thoughts, and feel free to add or remove traits from this list based on your own experiences.

After defining each characteristic, I pose a question to help you reflect on your capabilities in this particular area. Don't think of this as a scorecard. Rather, the goal is for you to reflect and then take an honest look at where you are right now. Not every leader will display all of these traits all the time. We are individuals, and we are humans. That means we have the gift of developing, growing, and changing.

Bold Leader Qualities

1. **Courageous.** Being bold is, by definition, being courageous. Without courage and confidence in your skills and abilities, you will not be able to move forward when confronting risks, take action in the face of uncertainty, or defend your ideas and values against critics. Remember, courage is not about the absence of fear or anxiety. It is the willingness to move forward despite fear because you know it's the right thing to do. When you act courageously, you show others the path ahead. You know you will be able to navigate uncertainty because of your preparation, your abilities, and your team.
   Ask yourself: *"Am I willing to stand alone?"*

2. **Persistent.** Despite what we see in movies and on TV, achievement rarely comes quickly. Even people who are "overnight successes" were usually working for years

before their big breakthrough, and they likely experienced many ups and downs along the way. In fact, your mission will probably look more like a marathon made up of inches rather than miles. Often, you must work tirelessly without obvious progress or through setbacks, fueled by your belief that success will come ... eventually. When you demonstrate persistence and resilience, you demonstrate hope and that failure is something to learn from, not avoid.

Ask yourself: *"Do I embrace the process, or do I look only for the result?"*

3. **Decisive.** Some research estimates that we make an astounding 35,000 decisions each and every day.[18] Great leaders know that some decisions require more research and care than others. They save their time and energy for important topics, then make the call, even in the face of incomplete information and uncertainty. They know that it is often easier to deal with the results of what turns out to be a "wrong" choice than it is to recover from a delay.

Ask yourself: *"Can I make tough decisions quickly and deal with the results?"*

4. **Acts on Faith.** I believe it's impossible to handle the uncertainty of undertaking a challenging mission without faith. My belief in God underlies everything I do as a leader and guides my journey. I act on this faith when

I move forward, trusting that the passion in me was placed there by my creator. Without faith, we can feel rudderless and lost. With faith, we can trust in something larger than ourselves.

Ask yourself: *"Do I believe that I am here for a purpose?"*

5. **Humble.** Even the most powerful leaders are teachable and willing to defer to experts when the situation calls for it. Great people know what they know — and they know what they *don't* know. As a result, they ask for input from others when necessary. You can be both humble and confident because your goal is to impact others, not to receive glory yourself. Humility recognizes that you and your team are working in service of a larger purpose, and moving forward is more important than getting credit.

Ask yourself: *"Am I willing to step back in order to move forward?"*

6. **Resourceful.** Just as remodeling a home always takes more time and money than you think it will, launching your dream will also take more resources than you anticipate. Great leaders make the most of what they have and also know that sometimes the best results come when you find creative ways to do more within your limits. The most innovative ideas can come from constraints because you are forced to think through all possibilities to find the most effective one.

Ask yourself: *"In what ways do I challenge myself to do more with less?"*

7. **Principled.** When someone's personality, values, or priorities seem to change on a daily basis, it's hard to trust them — or follow them. That's why strong leaders are principled in that they stand for something. They don't waver. Because they're consistent from day to day, others are willing to come alongside them because they trust the direction that's being set. No one has to guess at your motivations because you display them so clearly in your words and deeds. Ask yourself: *"Is what I stand for clear to everyone around me?"*

8. **Focused.** Many bold leaders are "ideas" people with more opportunities than they can pursue. The ability to focus on one clear outcome at a time allows you to progress more quickly and also maximizes resources and momentum. It creates trust in others, as they're not trying to follow ever-changing goals and priorities. Ask yourself: *"Am I clear on my goals and priorities?"*

9. **Forward-thinking.** While managers are responsible for allocating resources in the present to meet current goals, leaders are visionaries thinking about what is yet to be created. Most bold plans focus on what is needed for the

future, and bold leaders think about how to address not yet realized scenarios and situations. Their mission drives themselves and their teams to a future goal that most people have not even imagined.

Ask yourself: *"Is my mission future-proof?"*

10. **Insightful.** Gathering data and information before making a decision is an essential leadership skill. Equally critical, though, is taking the next step and seeing beyond the details to understand what the research actually means in order to make decisions that are best aligned with your goals. The best leaders can discern between what is important and what is not; then, they decide accordingly.

Ask yourself: *"Am I able to interpret research and data to make effective decisions?"*

11. **Anticipatory.** Anticipatory people are those who can see a logical chain of events that move forward from a single point in time. This is similar to how chess Grandmasters play out entire games in their heads based on the single move of the first pawn. By anticipating potential pitfalls, objections, and concerns, great leaders can answer questions before they arise and garner needed resources ahead of time.

Ask yourself: *"Do I foresee issues and problems and plan for them before they occur?"*

12. Passionate. To move forward despite risk and fear, you must have a burning desire that motivates you. Passionate leaders are those who feel deeply about the cause they're working toward or the people they're working for. They are driven by something greater than themselves. When others sense that depth of commitment and emotion, they are moved as well.

Ask yourself: *"How deeply am I committed to my mission?"*

13. Driven. Commitment and passion lead to drive. Leaders with a bold mission see their objectives as "must-haves" rather than "nice-to-haves." Achieving their goals and impacting others is imperative, and they are willing to make themselves uncomfortable and take risks in order to succeed. It's this drive that motivates them to work hard, even when the rewards are slow in coming.

Ask yourself: *"Is my success optional or essential?"*

14. Comfortable with Risk. Moving into unknown territory is, by definition, risky. Many people won't face that risk, or they'll allow it to paralyze them. Others, though, can maintain a level head and face uncertainty head-on. The most effective leaders are comfortable taking calculated risks, trusting in their preparation and judgment. They know the reward will be worth the discomfort.

Ask yourself: *"Am I able to take calculated risks when necessary?"*

15. **Innovative.** Effective leaders assess the terrain ahead and devise a route to get from where they are to where they dream of going. That means they often create new solutions that have yet to be tested. Bold missions require going where there is no path. Sometimes, instigating change is the best way to advance a mission.

Ask yourself: *"Do I create new solutions to existing problems?"*

The 16th Trait

Are you looking over those 15 items and thinking it's a tall order to embody all these characteristics simultaneously? If so, please note that "perfection" was nowhere on the list! You're human. Leadership is dynamic, and you won't always get it right. We learn from our missteps and adjust as we move forward. Over time, you'll learn to trust your instincts.

The importance of instinct is why I want to talk about what I believe is the single most important characteristic a bold leader needs to exhibit — integrity. You might call integrity your conscience. As a Christian, I refer to it as the Holy Spirit. It's an inner compass that points you toward the right thing to do. When you do the right thing at the right time, you're acting with integrity.

Let's look at the definition of integrity. There are actually a few definitions. The first is perhaps the most known and defines integrity as the "firm adherence to a code of especially moral or artistic values." But a second definition is equally important: "the quality or state of being complete or undivided : completeness."[19]

When you look over the list of leaders you admire, I imagine they are all people of integrity. Not every decision they made turned out as they wished, but they acted in accordance with their conscience and their values. They were the same whether they were talking to a homeless person or a millionaire. They were truly whole.

For us to emulate iconic leaders, we also must be people of integrity, meaning we speak up when our conscience and values require us to, even if it's against the common narrative or PC culture. Integrity means being willing to risk criticism and even rejection for standing up for what you know is right and what you believe in.

Acting in accordance with your values is a shortcut to all the other traits on this list. In any given situation, instead of running through a list of 20 different traits, you can simply say, "How do I now act as a person of integrity?" That will force you to pause and look inward. At this moment, listen to what your conscience says and act accordingly. That path will never steer you wrong. If you can lay your head on your pillow at the end of the day knowing you acted with integrity, you've done the right thing.

In the Old Testament, the Psalmist writes, "But you have upheld me because of my integrity, and set me in your presence forever" (Psalm 41:12, ESV).

PART FOUR WRAP-UP

Anyone with a big purpose in their heart has the desire to impact others. After all, it's rare to put extensive resources and effort into a project if we don't expect to see positive returns on our investments.

But before you can impact others, you must *believe* that you are the one to put this dream into action. You must *own* your role as a leader, and then you must *live* out your purpose in your daily life. That's when you begin to see your efforts come to fruition. And that's when you must start thinking about imparting the lessons you've learned to others so they can *duplicate* them and believe, own, and live their own bold mission.

An acorn grows into an oak tree over many years. As it matures, it then spreads its own seeds that will, in turn, become trees with acorns of their own. The cycle continues for the oak and for you as you inspire and lead others to embrace and act on what's in their own hearts.

That is the natural progression of a leader. That is also the process we've been charting in this book as you learn how to move forward with your mission. What I want to impress on you is that your leadership lies not only in those you have helped directly but also in the example you've set for others to follow. What kinds of leaders will you develop or inspire?

Chapter 14

Leaving Your Legacy

When I retired from my corporate career, I had spent three decades building, mentoring, leading, connecting, and encouraging my colleagues and team members. Whether as a new agent or a high-level executive on the national level, I knew it was a role I was meant to play. What I didn't know, though, was the true impact of what I'd poured my heart and soul into for so many years. My reward came from the knowledge that I'd done my best nearly every step of the way, and that was enough for me.

That's why I was absolutely floored at what happened when I announced I was retiring.

When someone leaves an executive position after a significant period of time, the human resources department asks if you'd like an email to be sent to the entire company with an invitation to share memories or well wishes with the soon-to-be-departed. I wasn't sure I wanted to do the "grand exit." I figured I'd simply fade away quietly.

Of course, I thought I'd be missed for a while, but soon my team would report to another executive, and my email would be redirected to another person. Nature abhors a vacuum, and spaces left are quickly filled, especially on a Fortune 50 organizational chart. There's just too much going on, and things move too quickly for the world to stop turning because one person in the giant network steps aside. I had no illusions about being irreplaceable or even being remembered beyond the occasional text or Christmas card.

At the same time, though, I felt that inviting others to share their thoughts was a sign of respect to those I'd worked with, letting them in on the process of saying goodbye and offering them closure after working together for so many years. With that in mind, I finally gave the go-ahead to HR to send the email. I thought maybe I'd receive a handful of stories thanking me for a presentation I gave at our annual meeting or in appreciation of a long-term mentoring relationship.

What I got instead was two binders full of notes, cards, emails, and reminders that we are always leading and always impacting others — regardless of job title and regardless of whether you know it or not. Yes, I received the expected thank yous from close colleagues and team members, but they were far outnumbered by the recollections and appreciation for encounters I didn't even remember:

*"Debra, I will never forget that conversation we had
    in the elevator ..."*
*"You probably don't remember this, but you changed
    the course of my career over lunch ..."*
"Thank you so much for your wise advice ..."
*"Your encouragement came exactly when I needed
    it most ..."*

Story after story, card after card, and email after email re-counted conversations in passing that barely made a blip on my radar but that had deeply impacted others.

I tell you this not as a sign of my importance but as a re-minder of *yours*. Believe me when I tell you that you are always impacting those around you — positively or negatively, for good or bad, and whether you know it or not. You are always leading, no matter what your job title says.

As I look back on my career, I am so thankful for the times when I stewarded my leadership well. I can't help but wonder, though, what I might have done if I'd realized that while the "official" moments of leadership were important, The times off the stage and out of the spotlight were even more critical. What could I have done if I'd been more in-tentional and known that I was always leading and that ev-ery conversation mattered?

That is what I want for you: Strive to harness your strengths, skills, experience, and passion more intentionally and direct it toward the areas in which you feel called to serve ... toward your bold mission.

Breaking Through Hesitation

As you've read this book, I hope you've taken the time to think, reflect, and feel the emotions that have arisen along the way. If you have, you've probably felt in turns excited, hopeful, and a bit daunted at the idea of recognizing the seed of purpose within you, bringing it out into the sunlight, watering it, and allowing it to take root and grow. If so, it's completely natural to experience a wide variety of thoughts and feelings. We can be inspired at the same time we're anxious and motivated at the same time we're hesitant.

After all, there is so much unknown about the process of growing a dream. Will the roots stretch deep enough to bring the needed stability? Will our little green shoot be able to withstand the heat and cold of others' expectations and criticisms? How much time and care will it take? What will other people say about it? What if we think we're planting a small plot of tomatoes, and instead, we end up with a huge pumpkin patch that invades and absorbs everything in its path? What about the fertilizer bills ... the water bills ... the time it will take to tend and nurture this new life? What if, after all our input and nurturing, it just shrivels and dries up? What if we end up with something we hadn't anticipated, and now we aren't sure what to do with it?

While these are legitimate concerns, I want to remind you of what we discussed back in chapter 5 when we talked about excuses. Perhaps your biggest "what ifs" might be, "What if I don't do this? What if I just take this little seed and put it back in the dark where no one notices?" Tempting as it may be, these are the most dangerous "what ifs" of all. They're misplaced ideas of safety that make us believe we are better off staying small, not risking, not growing, and not leading.

When I think back to my very early career days when I was deciding if I should stay the course, get yet another degree in education and move into higher administrative levels, or cash out my retirement and attempt to launch my own business in the insurance industry, I didn't know how it would turn out. Would I lose everything, or would my business become a success? I had no idea that those binders full of impactful moments with others awaited me.

Yet something inside of me was pulling me away from the path I thought I'd wanted and toward the unknown. I could no longer ignore the enticing lure of what could be. If I hadn't stepped out in faith, I'm sure my life still would have had many highs and many important conversations and interactions. But part of me would always have wondered what would have happened if I'd had the confidence and courage to answer the call of what could be. I'm so thankful that I don't have to live with the pain of regret.

What's Next

As we reach the end of our time together, it's important to think about where you will go from here. I sincerely hope that you will put the material in this book to work on your own courageous path. While I've laid out the overview for you, you must be the one to move forward, even if the entire journey is not yet clear. I believe that when you take that first step, however small, the next step will become clear.

Maybe for you, the first step is to believe that you're meant for something more. If so, then it's time to start digging to find out what that "more" might be — taking a look at your values, passions, skills, and experiences and seeing where they might lead you. You need to determine where you intersect with the needs of the world. That's where **Part One - Believe It** will assist you.

Or you might need a dose of confidence to own the purpose that is already crystal clear in your heart and mind. You know what you were meant to do, but you're hesitant to admit it because it will require you to say goodbye to where you are in order to move into something different and unknown. If so, head to **Part Two - Own It**.

Perhaps you're all-in on your mission, but you have to start making it real. If you need assistance assessing your resources and creating a support net to advise you and hold you accountable, or if you feel hampered by obstacles or the fear of failure, **Part Three - Live It** will help you.

Are you well into living your purpose and want to know what's next? It may be time for you to start thinking about inspiring others on their own bold missions. You can go to **Part Four - Duplicate It** for ideas on creating a positive ripple effect on other courageous individuals who are ready to step up.

While there is a framework you can follow, don't expect your path to look exactly like someone else's. Bold missions come in all shapes and sizes. For one person, your purpose may be to start a community food bank. For someone else, it may be to get a degree in nutrition and start counseling others who want to improve their health and wellness. For another, you may feel called to launch an organic juice company. Remember all the stories you've read about in this book; no two are the same, and that's wonderful. That is the beauty of finding and following your path. It doesn't need to look like anyone else's.

Wherever you are, you just need to take one more step forward. That's how bold missions are lived, one step at a time.

Your Commission

Regardless of your religion or political party, I think we can all agree that there is much work to do. Everywhere I look these days, I see a world calling out for sanity, intentionality, compassion, and strength. I see a world yearning for someone to lead them with passion, grit, and grace. In the absence of these kinds of leaders, people — especially younger generations — will follow anyone with a plan and a voice, for good or for bad. They need people who are willing to go beyond their own self-interest. They need people who are willing to stand up for what's right, even if it's not popular.

A quick review of history will show that great leaders were usually not those who said the popular thing and added their voices to the approved narrative. Courageous people aren't necessarily those with millions of followers on Instagram or subscribers on YouTube. Instead, they are the ones who said what needed to be said and did what needed to be done, regardless of how others viewed their actions. Brave leaders don't lead based on popular opinion: They lead from an inner sense of values and an unwavering focus on the end goal.

If there is one thing I want to leave you with, it's the need to be intentional about how you live your days. Whether or not you choose to say yes to the unknown, you will always be leading and impacting others. The only choice is *how* we will lead. What will your answer be?

Whatever you choose, I pray you move forward with intention, grace, purpose, and love. I leave you with the words of the Apostle Paul:

> *As a prisoner for the Lord, then, I urge you to live a life worthy of the calling you have received. Be*

completely humble and gentle; be patient, bearing with one another in love. Make every effort to keep the unity of the Spirit through the bond of peace.

–Eph. 4:1-3, NIV

Author's Note

When I retired a few years ago, many people urged me to write a book. My initial reaction was, "Who really wants to read another book on leadership? What do I have to share that's meaningful enough to impact others' lives?" But as I started speaking at conferences and coaching individuals, I saw firsthand how many people were searching for help to improve themselves and their careers.

At the same time, my concern about our world was increasing. All around me, I saw chaos, uncertainty, and fear. There was a desperate need for strong leaders who could influence change. More specifically, I saw a need for BOLD leaders who would stand up for the truth, even if it was an unpopular stance.

As I reflected on my experiences as an executive for 24 years, I realized that two elements contributed to my success in leading others. First, my commitment to doing what's right, no matter the consequences. Second, my belief in the intrinsic value of others. Both of these come directly from my Christian faith, which has provided me with a strong foundation that has allowed me to take risks and stand up for my beliefs. Over the years, I became known as a BOLD leader because of my unwavering defense of the truth and the people for whom I was responsible.

Consequently, as I considered writing this book, I wanted to encourage boldness in leaders. I knew my audience was made up of people who would stand by their principles. People who would embrace boldness as they pursued their calling, despite the challenges that inevitably arise in pursuit of significance. I believe these leadership skills are what will make a difference in the future.

I hope you enjoy this book, the individuals we highlight, and the stories of how these individuals courageously pursued their dreams!

In boldness,
Debra

Resources

Books

Grace Meets Grit: How to Bring Out the Remarkable, Courageous Leader Within by Diana Middleton

Truth Changes Everything by Dr. Jeff Myers

For Such a Time as This by Kayleigh McEnany

A Mother's Grace: Healing the World One Woman at a Time by Michelle Moore

Change Your Culture, Change Everything: The Leader's Guide to Organizational Transformation by Samuel Chand

8 Steps to Achieve Your Destiny: Lead Your Life with Purpose by Samuel Chand

Bigger, Faster Leadership: Lessons from the Builders of the Panama Canal by Samuel Chand

Leadership Pain: The Classroom for Growth by Samuel Chand

Education and Coaching

Jorgensen Learning Center - Ray Jorgensen
   https://www.gojlc.com/
   Executive and leadership coaching as well as monthly webinars
DebraBoblitt.com
Mindhelm - Gina Yanovich
   Gina@mindhelm.org

Services

Dr. Nathan Goodyear
   https://brio-medical.com
Pearl Med Spa
   Pearlmedspa.com
   1339 NW Couch St. Portland, OR 97209
   7144 E Stetson Dr, Suite C-210
   Scottsdale, AZ 85251
Mother's Grace
   https://mothers-grace.org/
House of Nailz - Owner, Ericka Rosas
   @Houseof_nailz

About the Author

Business coach and speaker Debra Boblitt spent decades as an executive with a Fortune 50 financial services company. She served as senior vice president before leaving the organization to pursue a portfolio career, including coaching individuals and speaking to groups of all sizes.

She has a proven track record of increasing revenue and market share, developing dynamic teams, and leading through change. As senior vice president with full P&L responsibilities for a $3 billion market, she improved the organization's profit margin by 5.5 percent. Additional areas of expertise include customer needs and behaviors, and marketing and distribution. During her time as a corporate executive, she was known for her bold leadership combined with unwavering integrity and a heart for her team.

Debra speaks on a variety of topics for audiences big and small. It was always her dream to make a positive impact in the lives of others. She shares her insights on leadership while inspiring, motivating, and challenging people from all different backgrounds. Combining a strategic approach with an innovative perspective, Debra helps people break through barriers and challenges, overcome doubts, and take the necessary steps toward achieving their goals.

To get in touch or to find out more about working with Debra, including coaching and speaking engagements, visit DebraBoblitt.com.

Endnotes

1   Kierkegaard, S., *Selections from the Writings of Kierkegaard*, trans. L. M. Hollander, Project Gutenberg, accessed October 29, 2022, https://www.gutenberg.org/fils/60333/60333-h/60333-h.htm.

2   Barna, G., *New Insights into the Generation of Growing Influence: Millennials In America*, Phoenix, AZ: Cultural Research Center at Arizona Christian University and Foundations of Freedom, 2021.

3   Clifton, J., *State of the Global Workplace: 2021 Report*, Washington, DC: Gallup, 2021, https://www.gallup.com.

4   Longfellow, Henry Wadsworth, "A Psalm of Life," Poetry Foundation, accessed October 29, 2022, https://www.poetryfoundation.org/poems/44644/a-psalm-of-life.

5   *Merriam-Webster*, "Excuse definition & meaning," accessed July 19, 2022, https://www.merriam-webster.com/dictionary/excuse.

6 *Merriam-Webster,* Impact definition & meaning, accessed August 19, 2022, https://www.merriam-webster.com/dictionary/impact

7 Clark, N., "Simulators train aircrew at fraction of cost," US Air Force, accessed August 25, 2022, https://www.af.mil/News/Article-Display/Article/500033/simulators-train-aircrew-at-fraction-of-cost/#:~:text=Students%20spend%20136.5%20hours%20in,and%20only%2035%20hours%20flying.

8 *Merriam-Webster,* "Obstacle definition & meaning," accessed August 22, 2022, https://www.merriam-webster.com/dictionary/obstacle.

9 *Merriam-Webster,* "Mistake definition & meaning," accessed August 22, 2022, https://www.merriam-webster.com/dictionary/mistake.

10 *Merriam-Webster,* "Failure definition & meaning," accessed August 22, 2022, https://www.merriam-webster.com/dictionary/failure.

11 *Merriam-Webster,* "Mentor definition & meaning," accessed August 31, 2022, https://www.merriam-webster.com/dictionary/mentor.

12 *Merriam-Webster,* "Champion definition & meaning," accessed August 31, 2022, https://www.merriam-webster.com/dictionary/champion.

13 *Merriam-Webster,* "Coach definition & meaning," accessed August 31, 2022, https://www.merriam-webster.com/dictionary/coach.

14 *Merriam-Webster,* "Net definition & meaning," accessed August 31, 2022, https://www.merriam-webster.com/dictionary/net.

15 Prodanoff, J. T., "How many ads do we see a day? 17 insightful stats from 2022," WebTribunal, May 16, 2022, https://webtribunal.net/blog/how-many-ads-do-we-see-a-day/#gref.

16 Cohn-Sheehy, Brendan I. et al., "The hippocampus constructs narrative memories across distant events," *Current Biology* 31, no. 22, (November 2021): 4935-4945, DOI: 10.1016/j.cub.2021.09.013.

17 Montopoli, J., "Public speaking anxiety and fear of brain freezes," National Social Anxiety Center, January 31, 2021, https://nationalsocialanxietycenter.com/2017/02/20/public-speaking-and-fear-of-brain-freezes/.

18 Graff, F., "How many daily decisions do we make?" UNC, September 7, 2018, http://science.unctv.org/content/reportersblog/choices.

19 *Merriam-Webster,* "Integrity definition & meaning," accessed September 19, 2022, https://www.merriam-webster.com/dictionary/integrity.

Made in the USA
Middletown, DE
17 February 2024

49381410R00099